CW00525183

FADING INTO RETIREMENT

Francis Reid

ENTERTAINMENT TECHNOLOGY PRESS

Biographical Series

To my beloved wife Jo
our children Angus, Fiona and Catriona
their husbands Steve and James
and our grandchildren Kayleigh, Marcus, Frankie and Edie

Cover image: "Slowly restored to a stable 'normality' with reduced mobility." – The author with Zimmer frame.

FADING INTO RETIREMENT

Francis Reid

To [handwritten dedication] with best wishes [signature]

etpress

Entertainment Technology Press

Fading into Retirement

© Francis Reid

First published November 2014
Entertainment Technology Press Ltd
The Studio, High Green, Great Shelford, Cambridge CB22 5EG
Internet: www.etnow.com

ISBN 978 1 904031 78 9

A title within the
Entertainment Technology Press Biographical Series
Series editor: John Offord

All rights reserved. No part of this publication may be reproduced in any material form (including photocopying or storing in any medium by electronic means and whether or not transiently or incidentally to some other use of this publication) without the written permission of the copyright holder except in accordance with the provisions of the Copyright, Designs and Patents Act 1988. Applications for the copyright holder's written permission to reproduce any part of this publication should be addressed to the publishers.

CODE / FiR01_11-14

CONTENTS

PROLOGUE

This is the final book in my fading trilogy which, with *Fading Light* and *Carry on Fading*, updates my *Hearing the Light* record of places visited, performances seen, and people met.

Never say never, but I use the 'final' label because decreasing mobility means that my ability to travel is diminished to the point that my life is now contained within a very few square miles.

My memories are triggered by over 600 CDs, half of them Handel and 100 or so DVDs supplemented by a rental subscription to LOVEFiLM.

Although no longer writing about the past and having no intention to speculate about the future, I may continue to record memories of the past.

Death, the ultimate unknown, is the only inevitable fact of life.

Jo and I have discussed it and agreed that neither of us is afraid of death – only the manner of it. Apart from living on through our deeds and our children, we have no expectation of an afterlife but are fully prepared to be surprised.

14 Fading into Retirement

OCTOBER 2010

Diaghilev

The curtain rises on this third volume of my fadebook with *DIAGHILEV and the Golden Age of the Ballets Russes 1909-1929* at the V & A. Blockbuster is a label often used with doubtful justification and although not marketed as such, this exhibition really does bust the blocks – both for the material and the way it is displayed. The path through the exhibition follows a timeline from the 1909 launch through the war years and the twenties to the legacy that remains a powerful influence on the visual and performing arts of today and – surely – also tomorrow. With figures like Bakst, Balanchine, Chanel, Cocteau, Fokine, Lifar, Massine, Matisse, Nijinsky, Picasso, Prokofiev and Stravinsky, how could it be otherwise? A largesse of Ballet Russe costumes provides continuity as the story unfolds through designs, drawings, photographs and ephemera, with Howard Goodall popping up on a series of screens to discuss the music. Scattered among the exhibits are examples of functioning period stage lighting equipment. Being from the thirties they may be marginally anachronistic but add to the ambience and trigger a whiff of nostalgia for the spill rings and cloud machines of my salad days. The Diaghilev era was a time when scenery was still décor and entrusted to painters. In addition to the designs, there is a full scale example: Picasso's frontcloth for *Le Train Bleu* – all 54 square metres of it – from 1924. Such 'scandals' as *The Rites of Spring* are well documented as are the financial traumas endemic in any avant garde theatre. Film is used extensively and a video montage explains inspiration in a way that words never can.

Radamisto

Enjoyable? Yes. Stimulating? Not very. The plot is clear and the characters credible – even if, unusually for a Handel opera, they are people who generate little sympathy for their predicament. Despite sitting in the third row (I like to get close when baroque opera is played in a cavern like the Coliseum) I feel no involvement in their problems while getting a lot of pleasure from their singing. The orchestra, silkily smooth almost to the point of blandness, accompany rather than enter into a dialogue with the voices. Are they happy in the pit tonight? Not on the evidence of their chug along phrasing. The setting is yet another of these unnecessarily expensive move-around-to-little-purpose jobs. Well, at least it does not get in the way of the actors even if they are occasionally upstaged by dominant wallpaper. I suspect it may look better from a few rows further back. All in all, a pleasant evening devoid of any risk taking. Certainly not an evening to forget – but not one to remember either.

Cuts

Today's much heralded review of public sending has been preceded by so many leaks to prepare us for a financial doomsday that there are few surprises. Expectations have increasingly overtaken resources to an unsustainable level and so we are all going to have to lower our sights. This will probably be easier for us oldies who have seen a growth in prosperity far beyond the aspirations of our youth. But, despite my indestructible optimism, I have to concede that the outlook is somewhat bleak.

NOVEMBER 2010

Fall back

The clocks have been put back and the russet leaves are falling. It is the first of November and winter may be approaching but it is a glorious late autumn day on the North Norfolk coast – clear skies over the salt marshes and enough sun to blush the flints of the cottages in Blakeney. The clear air stimulates my appetite for a fine piece of Haddock and a pint of Adnams at the Kings Head.

Fairies and sugar plums

It may be only early November but shortening days and a Nutcracker matinee at the Theatre Royal turn thoughts towards Christmas. Too early for my usual bout of panto withdrawal symptoms but they are decreasing year by year. Perhaps this afternoon's lovely wallow in transformations, star cloths and dry ice will provide some immunity.

Cool

A maltreated word is redefined by the Jumbo Captain who reports an engine blow out as "we have a technical issue". And confirms why the professionalism of pilots makes me a confident flier.

A Sheridan Opera

Will a revival of *The Duenna* be worth an overnight in Cambridge? A Covent Garden hit in 1775 with a first run of 75 performances, 12 more than *The Beggars Opera*, it has lain dormant since the 1840s until this revival by English Touring Opera. Worthwhile? An emphatic Yes. Sheridan's

English Touring Opera.

text provides a plot suitable for Donizetti or Rossini and if father and son Linley are not quite in that league, the score is a pleasant sequence of tunes in mostly ballad style. The plot depends on the extent to which a veil disguises a lady irrespective of her height and girth. But, if the deceived person is a buffo, suspension of this one small piece of disbelief is not a problem. Adam Wiltshire's rather elegant set sits well on the Arts Theatre stage, suggesting Bath rather than the Seville of the libretto. The period band are behind the set, unobtrusively visible, allowing the action to connect with the audience in the 18th century mode. Every single word – many of Sheridan's lines are as everlasting as those of Oscar Wilde – is projected with a rare clarity. I'd like to see and hear it again.

Dramma non giocoso

The latest Glyndebourne production has all the drama but little of the lightness implied by the giocoso of the label Dramma Giocoso that Mozart and da Ponte attached to their *Don Giovanni*. Dressed for the 1950s, but behaving with little of that period's formalities, the characters indulge in a series of inexplicable relationships. What do these ladies see in this uncharismatic yob of a Don Giovanni? Why does this Zerlina, an Essex girl engaged to a Masseto in a sharp suit that suggests a city trader, fall for him. Or Anna forsake an Ottavio who, for once, does not come over as a bit of a wimp? Only the unattached Elvira has some credibility – or would have if Giovanni just occasionally turned on a bit of fake charm. Which leaves Leporello. Why does he support a Giovanni who treats him thus? Da Ponte has written a master servant relationship as complex as the Cervantes portrayal of Don Quihotte and Sancho Panza.

Glyndebourne Don Giovanni "La ci darem".

Like Alfonso in *Cosi*, Leporello is a Mozartian upgrade of the traditional buffo. But tonight there is no cynicism, no admiration, no humour and above all, no subtlety. Or perhaps I just have a closed mind, tainted by memories of Geraint Evans and Sesto Bruscantini.

Monteverdi's *Poppea*

At the behest of Amore, the opera's sprightly deus ex machina, acres of red lush plush curtain swivel and track to contract, expand and shape the stage in opulent decadence. Three lutes, harp, organ, three recorders two harpsichords and eight strings add glorious textures as an eternal triangle moves inexorably through its cycle of misery-inducing passion towards a climax of unsustainable bliss. Ending the opera with a passionate love duet – one of opera's most meltingly ravishing expressions of love and sensuality – may satisfy Amore's prologue assertion to Virtu and Fortuna about the supremacy of love over morality and luck but history knows better. A tale so timeless that updating to any era including today is free from dodgy moments. Glyndebourne – on their annual visit to Norwich Theatre Royal – are back on form with the sure touch that eluded them in last night's Don Giovanni.

Having lit the 1962 production that restored *L'incoronazione di Poppea* to the repertoire, this was an evening of deja vu. Back then, Monteverdi operas were a crusade led by Raymond Leppard. From stage managing a 1958 John Cranko production of Leppard's edition of *Il hallo delle ingrate* at Aldeburgh, I had acquired a taste that grew exponentially during rehearsals – as indeed it did for all of us. We knew it was going to be a hit and it was. These were was early days for research into 17th and 18th century performance practice but for continuo we had two harpsichords, two organs, two celli, two basses, lute, guitar and harp. However, there was large body of strings playing in a 19th century style. No recorders but a pair of modern trumpets to herald the coronation. (I would later use the recording of this ritornello for the moment when the Mayor of Bury St Edmunds inaugurated the first memory lighting control in the Theatre Royal!). Night after night, with my finger on the slider to time the final fade to the final bar, my soul melted as I listened to Magda Laszlo and Richard Lewis sing the closing duet. Tonight Nerone is a mezzo and once again the tainted memory syndrome kicks in to feeds my preference for the voluptuous sound of Lewis and Laszlo.

Brook's Flute

Stripped back to their glorious essentials, Peter Brook's *Magic Flute* and his Theatre Bouffes du Nord are a marriage made for an operatic utopia. *Die Zauberflöte* is too complex for a definitive production and Brook acknowledges this with *Une Flute Enchanteé* – not '*The*' *Magic Flute* but '*A*' *Magic Flute*. Going straight to the core of the work with a breathtakingly lateral approach, he cuts the three ladies, boys and serpent. The stage is a bare space contracted and expanded, shaped and defined, by free-standing six foot poles positioned by the actors. Despite the cuts and some

Peter Brooke's A Magic Flute at Théâtre des Bouffes du Nord.

tampering – Papageno's 'Der Vogelfanger bin ich ja' becomes a duet with Tamino – Brook is faithful to the music. The arias are sung in German with French side titles while much of the the French dialogue is underscored with music drawn from elsewhere, particularly from the cuts. Making no attempt to orchestral pretension, the piano accompaniment is so sparse, clear and confident that it is easy to believe that Mozart has written a chamber opera for keyboard. Sarastro, so often something of a bore, is at last a real person as is Monostatos. The Queen of the night is a confused dysfunctional mother and when Papageno finally meets his Papagena their duet is accompanied by coitus (without any hint of interruptus) staged with beautiful discretion. Tamino is a young idealist and our hearts genuinely bleed for Pamina in 'Ach Ich Fuls'. Brook's many lateral shafts of imagination include a triangle in lieu of Papageno's magic bells – we know it is magic because the first ping triggers a momentary freeze – and the trials are staged so simply with delicate fire and water projections that they are totally believable. For an hour-and-a-half without interval there is no applause until the end when it bursts with an outpouring of joy and enlightenment. The audience are totally engrossed as if at a play. I am now closer to the work than I have ever been. I have seen dozens of magnificent productions and learned something more from each one. But Peter Brook provides a new insight that will colour all my future *Flutes*. I'd love to see a Bouffes du Nord *Cosi fan Tutte*.

Researching Craig

The reason I am in Paris (apart from the bread which is reason enough) is to study Edward Gordon Craig documents in the Arts du Spectacle department of the BnF (Bibliotheque Nationale de France). The story of why am I doing so begins with the 2008 SIBMAS Congress in Glasgow when an invitation led to a Paris visit to appraise the documents followed by a research award from the Society for Theatre Research (a tale that unfolds in pages 125,139,186 of *Carry on Fading*). While the old library

Edward Gordon Craig self-portrait.

on Rue Richelieu is undergoing massive restoration with many of its activities relegated to stacked portakabins, the performing arts reading room is camping in the 1645 splendours of the Mazarin Gallery. So I find myself, lit by a chandelier, working under a magnificent 17th century painted ceiling. Craig's papers are scattered around the world with a substantial collection in Paris including many that were unknown to Rood & Fletcher when they compiled their definitive bibliography in 1967.

One of these is the notebook that EGC kept from 1920 to 1941 to record details of the history of stage lighting that he uncovered in the course of his wide reading. Over the last few months I have been slowly transcribing a facsimile – not an easy task since his spidery 'u' 'm' and 'n' are so similar that it takes some acquaintance with lighting history to reach a decision based on context. Many of the references to French, German

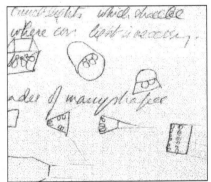

Craig's bunch lights predict LED luminaires.

and Italian authorities can only be resolved by experimentally entering alternative names into google. Now I make my final checks against the original which is a mite clearer than the facsimile and succeed in reducing the uncertainties to a mere half dozen words. While the book is peppered with interesting references to follow up, overall it offers considerable insight into the acquisitive mind that fed Craig's lateral thinking. In particular he comes across as a much more practical man of the theatre that is allowed by much 'received wisdom'.

This is reflected in many of the other documents in the BnF. His handwritten rehearsal notes are precisely those that any director might take today and the edited typed version would cause no surprise when e-mailed to the production team. His scene-by-scene analyses provide viable indicators to assist his lighting designer determine the role of light in the scenographic concept. There are costume designs ready to go to the cutter. It was not so much the lack of technology as the attitudes of the theatre establishment of his time that frustrated the fulfilment of his ideas. Just as he reached the end of his life, the technology began to flow but more significantly there was a seismic change of attitude. My generation were able to realise many of Craig's dreams. Where is the new Craig to signpost the future?

French Baroque

Somewhat belatedly, I am developing a taste for 18th century French opera. Although short excerpts of Lully and Rameau have long tickled my ears, whole operas have failed to enchant – even when researched and recorded on original instruments. But fascination has been triggered by recent DVDs of both creatively-updated and period-researched productions. The revival of *Cadmus et Hermione* at the Opéra Comique, a co-production with the Centre de Musique Baroque de Versailles, seeks to recreate the musical, acting, costume, scenic and lighting styles of the première. The result, stimulating and entertaining, brings us closer to an understanding of baroque opera and its staging. Chariots descend, the floor opens, dragons appear and are slain. Their scattered teeth immediate grow into warriors – and in the low flickering light the effect is magically real. More such productions are on the way and I have the six Parisian opera houses bookmarked alongside Eurostar.

Is it that time already?

The title of Rikki Fulton's autobiography neatly describes the way that a fade can be so smooth that its progress is imperceptible until some event triggers an awareness of the relentless progression of time. Two Norwich theatres, the Playhouse and the Puppet theatre, are celebrating anniversaries. Having served on the Boards of both from the later stages of

Rikki Fulton in A Wish for Jamie.

their gestation, through their building to their opening, I am hit by a wave of tempus fugit on realising that they are 15 and 30 years old respectively. I was in Paris during the Puppet celebrations but I am at the Playhouse to nibble the birthday, drink the mulled wine and join in the reminiscences triggered by the ephemera exhibited throughout the foyers. Time has been kind to the building. Performers and audience like it and that is very comforting when remembering how squeezy-tight budgeting demanded particularly rigid assessment of priorities.

DECEMBER 2010 – JANUARY 2011

Stricken by the Ides of March

Jack Schofield's Guardian computer column once warned that *data doesn't really exist unless you have two copies of it. Preferably more. And the only person who can be held responsible for that is you.* In theory my scribblings are adequately stored, not just in two but three places: hard drive, disc or stick, and printout. Well that's the theory and so, when I discover that the file of this journal has succumbed to my butterfingers, I am not immediately concerned. I run a search that tells me it is no longer in my hard drive but saved on the back-up disc of the week before last. Alas my back-up disc is rewritten weekly. Then I discover that I never got around to setting up a dedicated disc or stick when I started this volume. And the printout? Well that fizzles out before Christmas. So, after scanning the October and November entries, I now have to reconstruct the last three months. The essence of my scribblings, written in the present tense, is noting reactions of the moment. So, using the past tense, all I can do now is attempt a recall.

The lost months

Despite the persistent ice that marked the run up to Christmas, I made it to London for seasonal gatherings missed for the past two years. The ABTT assembled in the grand salon of Drury Lane. Us oldies were out in force. But where were the youth of the parish? Working on pantomime matinees? Staging seasonal soirées for bankers? Or perhaps they question the relevance of such a forum to today's theatre? When the ABTT was young, such meetings were alive with the energy of young arti-anarchical youth. Now they are reunions of the established and the retired.

The ALD (formerly the SBTD) is also 50-years-old but its annual lighting lunch attracted a mix across the generations including the eager young thrusters – despite the ABTT lunch being free but the lighting one 50 quid. I enjoyed my two sessions of good cheer with lots of reminiscence tempered by some tentative speculation about the future.

Not much to recall of the festive season itself except that it was chilly outside and cosy within as we enjoyed the established family rituals. If I made any New Year Resolutions, I don't remember what they were.

In January our Theatre Royal hosted a week of ballet from St Petersburg and we enjoyed afternoons of *Swan Lake* and *Sleeping Beauty*. The cloths may have been a bit frayed but the dancers had Petipa in their DNA and the orchestra had Tchaikovsky in theirs.

Otherwise, much of the wintry months have been spent trying to knock my archives into some sort of state for deposit in the library of RSAMD. A slow process as I shuffle old plans, contacts, letters and ephemera that have lain dormant for several decades. Memories have been jogged, mostly pleasant but a few less so. A motley but detailed collection of paperwork that offers snapshot of a half century of backstage in general and lighting in particular. My instinct is to bin the lot but, who knows, some future historian may find interest in such a detailed primary source.

FEBRUARY 2011
Back to the present
At this points my scribbled notes remain so I can legitimately return to the present tense.

Opera pub
The King's Head in Islington, so long a fringe powerhouse for plays and musicals, has morphed into an opera house playing an extended season. With barely 100 seats and a vestigial stage, *Opera Up Close* is an appropriate name for the company presenting 8 performances a week from an expanding repertoire of six operas. Entrances are frequently made through the auditorium and duets sung across the audience from one aisle to the other. Every word of Tony Britten's witty new translation of *Cenerentola* is clear. My memory of Rossini's score is so detailed that the piano heard by my ear is orchestrated by my brain. Scenery, props and costumes may only be indicative but the characters are well developed and the ensemble strong. The interval is brought forward so

that the 'ballroom' scene can be played in the bar with audience joining the pub customers in partying with the singers who leap on and off tables and chairs as the action moves around the room. Cinderella arrives by bike (courtesy of Barclays Cycle Hire) and the act ends with all the zest of a Rossini crescendo. If this is not the ultimate in operatic outreach, what is?

Breathing in Karlsruhe

With every few yards requiring a pause for breath, the crucial prop for last year's Karlsruhe Festival was a Ventolin inhaler. No such problems today as I set off for the opening concert of three Handel concerti grossi interspersed with suites by Roman, and Galliard plus a bonne bouche of the *Alcina* ballet music. Conducted by Lars Erik Mortenesen, the most swooping and scooping physical harpsichordist I have ever seen, the 23 strings, four oboes and two bassoons of the Deutsche Handel Solisten dance lightly but profoundly. After three – or was it four – encores the applause continues until after the last musician has left the stage.

Billiard Battle

Operatic fights are difficult to stage, especially when armies are involved. Although Handel acknowledged the limitations of thrust and parry by keeping his battle music short but rousing, there remains considerable risk of raising an audience titter. Tonight the concentric rings of the Statstheater's huge revolve deliver two billiard tables so that combat to be decided by cues and balls – just one short scene in a lavishly staged *Partenope*. In the pit, with no less than three lutes, are the Deutsche Handel Solisten conducted by Michael Hofstetter who never fails to phrase to my liking. One good tune after another, sung by characters whom director Ulrich Peters has chosen to present as real humans rather than the caricatures so frequently favoured by directors who hear without listening.

Haydn in Cairo

There is a camel and a swimming pool on the revolve of Wuppertal Opernhaus for *L'Incontro Improviso* (*The Unexpected Encounter*). Responding to the 18th century fashion for opera with a Turkish flavour, Haydn sets the action in Egypt and this production, gently stressing Islamic elements, updates by a couple of centuries. Performed in a German translation as *Unverhofft in Kairo* (*Unexpected in Cairo*), the secco recitative is spoken but underscored by an Ud. (The Pascha speaks Turkish with German supertitles). The plot has strong resonances with

Unverhofft in Kairo at Opernhaus Wuppertal.

Mozart's *Seraglio* although this is a contemporary Islam where the belly dancing is tourist-oriented and hijabs are discarded to reveal swimsuits in the absence of men. The tunes are good and the comedy gentle. An enjoyable evening and worth the detour. Received wisdom assures us that Haydn operas are not dramatic – well, they once said that about Handel.

MARCH 2011

Dicky Ticker

Six monthly visit to the cardiac clinic confirms that my daily diuretic cocktail is continuing to compensate for the constrictions imposed on my circulation by the thickened pericardium that led to my hospitalisation last year.

Vivaldi

The restorers have been at work in St George's Hanover Square and by leaving well alone – just tidying up, painting and gilding – they have done a splendid job. Their old parishioner, G.F. Handel, would be well pleased. The more I sit in 18th century churches, the more I feel that the Gothic revival was something of an architectural and ecclesiastical blip. This year's London Handel Festival opens with a lunchtime Vivaldi concert by Trinity Laban Baroque. The continuous rise in the quality of student playing has been one of the great advances of my lifetime. But the axe hanging over cultural funding includes a likely chop for instrumental lessons in schools – there is an old established Westminster maxim that philistinism takes precedence.

Cod & Chips
The restorers have also been active in the pub at the vestry door and with much relief I find that it too has been tidied up rather than given the ghastly makeover which has afflicted so many of our traditional hostelries. And their battered cod is as splendid as ever it was.

Rodelinda
This year's London Handel Festival opera at the Royal College of Music, sung by postgraduate students with an orchestra of baroque professors, has gone mainstream with *Rodelinda* rather than pursue its usual exploration of more neglected works. This tale of love and intrigue in the corridors of power easily updates from mediaeval Lombardy to contemporary police states. Combining the roles of director and designer may not necessarily ensure harmony between actor and environment: this is dependent upon a well-balanced creative tension within the individual – no one is more conscious of designer-director creative tensions than their lighting designers who have to resolve the conflicting demands of scene and performer. But David Fielding, cast in this difficult role tonight, delivers a staging faithful to the libretti and sympathetic to the music. Alas, this music is poorly paced – continuously driven forward with little attempt at phrasing or caressing. An evening of many stirring moments but few melting ones.

Cinders in the blitz
Covered in plaudits, Matthew Bourne's *Cinderella* arrives for a sold out week in Norwich and lives up to all the praise that has been lavished. At the height of the London Blitz, Cinderella parties at the Café de Paris where she is traumatised by a midnight bombing raid during

Northern Ballet Theatre in Cinderella.

which she loses her slipper. But her Battle of Britain fighter pilot, searching the streets from the embankment to the underground, finally finds her in hospital, and as they leave Paddington Station with a 'just married' suitcase, her guardian angel finds another downtrodden girl to transform. With the classic stepsisters and stepmother augmented by an extended family of stepbrothers, boyfriends and girlfriends, there are lots of opportunities for the witty choreography that Matthew Bourne excels in.

Opening in a cinema showing period newsreels and evolving through nine locations, scene change continuity effected by transformations involving classic panto tricks from gauze to hinged collapses, the show is brilliantly designed by Lez Brotherston and lit by Neil Austin – there are few greater challenges for a lighting designer than London in a blackout. All that is missing is a live orchestra – Bourne makes a persuasive argument for a cinematic surround sound but, despite the quality of the 87 player specially recorded soundtrack, its loudness makes it obtrusive rather than integral. Oh dear, I really am a bit of a fogey when it comes to keeping theatre live!

Spring forward

The clocks move forward amid signs that winter is reluctantly making way for spring. Time was when I was rather good at winter and enjoyed its chilly challenges – especially on a crisp morning. Then I could rely on a body thermostat that was fine tuned by Edinburgh's 'wind up the Waverley steps' to adjust me to seasonal change. Now there is too much rust in my physiology to handle wide temperature variations – especially in a climate that has gone doolally. Bring me sunshine – but no heatwaves.

APRIL 2011

Der Rosenkavalier

May 30th 1965. Jo is six months pregnant with Catriona. I am sitting at the lighting desk in the production box at Glyndebourne. The opera is *Der Rosenkavalier* – a revival of the Carl Ebert 1959 production designed by Oliver Messel that marked my Glyndebourne début. I was not the lighting designer – that role was fulfilled by Peter Ebert – but with the newly coined title of lighting manager, I was within earshot of the production desk and party to the interactions of the creative team. The 1965 revival was what the Germans call a neueinstudierung, a new production in old sets. Not that Hans Neugebauer could depart radically from the Ebert staging – Messel sets and costumes do rather dictate a production style. And although that also applies to some extent to the lighting, Neugebauer and I shared ideas that would take advantage of the technology that had replaced the 1934 installation inherited in 1959. So I had the opportunity to redesign. As with the other Messel revivals of the 60s, Oliver usually made fleeting appearances that were friendly, stimulating and educational while Charles Bravery was always on had to freshen the paint. A happy occasion that I am reliving with newly issued disc transfers made from the tapes of that May night so long ago. Caballé, Otto Edelmann, Zylis-Gara, Edith Mathis et al were and remain terrific. As does John Pritchard and the LPO at their best. I am even reasonably, if unusually, pleased with the quality of the lighting in the photos.

Moral contrasts

Saul is mature Handel but, unlike the restrained orchestration of his late operas, deploys a large band with trumpets and kettledrums integral rather than occasional. For the première he borrowed drums from the Tower of London and imported trombone players from Germany as they were in limbo between going out of fashion and being rediscovered. But the music is not all militant bravado – the score includes some of Handel's most melting moments for flute and harp. With very few da capos, the action moves forward faster than in the operas with their obligatory repeats demanded by Italian aria conventions. This being the old testament, the goodies are very good and the baddies very bad but, following Saul's defeat with its famous dead march, clever old Handel tempers the bloodthirsty drama with a gentle elegy.

Octogeriatric

Pink Champagne for my birthday. Eighty feels little different from 18. My waking thoughts are of *The Magic Flute* – the dialogue between Papageno and Papagena (disguised as an old woman). "How old are you?" he asks. "Achtzehn jahre und zwei minuten" says she. "Acht**zig** jahre und zwei minuten," he muses. Nein, Nein! She replies "Acht**zehn** Jahre und Zwei minuten," I may be older but I am no wiser. The world which I was going to change is in an even worse mess than I found it.

Mozart's Titus

La Clemenza di Tito was Mozart's last opera but his first to reach London. Although remaining in the repertoire for 50 years after his death, it was the last mature opera to be revived during his twentieth century reinstatement as a major composer for the theatre. In the absence of performances, received wisdom grew into a dossier of misinformation about a work that is full of pointers to the future that were recognised by its initial audiences who thrived on novelty but ignored by the pedantry of later musicologists who regarded Mozart's Titus as a reversion to the old opera seria from which he had moved on. Letting my speculation run riot, could the opera's early success possibly have been helped by a hero showing clemency in the spirit of the age of enlightenment before it became unfashionable in the subsequent shift to materialism? But why speculate? Just sit back, enjoy and be grateful that *La Clemenza di Tio* is now established. And there is much pleasure in English Touring Opera's singing and playing even if the stage pictures give little pleasure to the eye or support to the action. On the evening when I am celebrating my eight decades, it is appropriate that I have the opportunity to enjoy an opera in which Mozart looked back to show the way forward.

Coming out at 80

A letter to The Times:

> On my 80th birthday, I feel qualified and entitled to voice, for the first time in my life, my political opinions. I believe that the present coalition is the best thing that has happened to British politics in my lifetime. Nick Clegg is enabling David Cameron to follow a positive middle course free from the doctrinaire extremes of the right and the left.
>
> Although I have never been a party activist, I admit to a lifetime of unswerving voting for the liberals in all their various manifestations. I will continue to do so with renewed fervour but if the referendum results in a no vote, I shall feel unable to continue full support for the idea that Britain is a democracy.

It is not published.

Dining with Fellows

At the Garrick, surrounded by paintings of actors when scenes and machines were lit by oil, candle and gas, the Fellows of the ABTT celebrate its first 50 years. The table is round and we are but ten – just right for permutations of one-to-one conversations through dinner followed by general debate once the port is passing. We reminisce about the past and contemplate the future of an organisation that has been pivotal in providing a communication hub for all of us involved in a half-century of backstage technical revolution. The toast is proposed by Richard Pilbrow in whose office the inaugural meeting was held as that catalytic decade, the 60s, began.

Survival celebrated

Day three of my octo-week and, like the Queen, I am having an official birthday – conceived and organised by John Offord. On the invitation of ETP, ABTT, ALD and the Theatres Trust, with sponsorship from too many equipment manufactures to mention, 90 backstagers assemble to dine at the Savile Club where the Ballroom provides a setting that could serve for Act 2 of *Der Rosenkavalier* with a magnificent staircase for everyone to ascend from reception to dinner.

Rosco gobo for my 80th Birthday.

With lots of old friends turning up, it is all rather like having a memorial service while one is still alive to enjoy it ... And I now have an embarrassing idea of what's going to be in my obituaries! Appropriately, as the Savile is in the same street as the house where Handel lived from 1723 until his death in 1759, Morgana's aria from

Mark White, Chairman of ABTT, proposes a birthday toast.

Jo and I with Claire Fox at my birthday party.

Jo and I with Freddie Grimwood at the party.

the Act One finale of *Alcina* is sung for me by Katy Offord. Afterwards, everyone is given a copy of a special edition of *Carry on Fading*. Anyone wishing it signed has the opportunity of dropping something into a bucket for Light Relief and the contributions raise over £900. It is rather nice to be the excuse for such a gathering of the great and the good, the movers and the shakers, of the world of filaments, filters and faders. I am mind boggled, gob smacked, awestruck and proud.

Comus unmasqued

By 1745, when Handel was a guest of the Earl of Gainsborough at Exton Hall, the English masque had morphed into the semi-opera that was already overtaken by Italian opera. But the masque format lingered on with Thomas Arne having his first hit with a setting of John Milton's 1634 *Comus* at Drury Lane in 1738. While Handel was at Exton this version became the basis for an evening's entertainment performed by the Earl and his family. So he composed five new numbers – subsequently recycling them for later operas – and inserted other 'pops' from his earlier works. Rediscovery of this music stimulated the research that with, just a hint of speculation, has led to a reconstruction premièred tonight in Handel's old church, St George's Hanover Square. For a single performance in such a venue on the tight budget of a festival shunned by the Arts Council for 34 successful years, there can be no hint of the extravagant décor that was such a feature of the Masque genre. No romantically wild wood, no magnificent hall, no magic. In an update to 1940 and the blitz, Milton's virtuous lady is in the WVS, her brothers are air raid wardens, the spirits are nurses with wings, and magician Comus is in a white coat.

Does it work? Not really. The actors, whose programme biographies are much longer than the musicians, bring a wealth of experience of supporting roles in every television drama series as ever was. But, scripts in hand, their rendering of John Milton's verse becomes turgid and the arrival of each musical number is met by a silent but palpable sigh of audience relief. Musically a pleasant evening to remember, but, poetically and dramatically best forgotten. However, Laurence Cummings who conducted, is designated artistic director of the Göttingen Festival from next year; perhaps he will mount *Comus* with the more generous resources that he will then have at his disposal.

Dangerous chairs

The room in my Travelodge has no chair. Are they following Ryanair's revenue enhancement strategy and reclassifying the bedroom chair as a customer option? I consult reception. "All chairs have been removed from all bedrooms on orders from Head Office." "Why?" "Health and safety." I did not imagine this. Indeed I could not have imagined it.

Street party

Stuart Road Royal Wedding street party.

A bank holiday for a royal wedding. I have often seen pictures of street parties on royal occasions but this is the first time that the iconic trestle table has been set up in the street where I live. The traditional union jack bunting is rather more restrained than in the old photos, while the obligatory beer, lemonade and buttys are swamped by the chilled champagne, pinot grigio, organic juices, prawns, dips, quiches and tossed salads relayed from the fridges and ovens of the Australians, Poles and diverse ethnic minorities who have organised this celebration of constitutional monarchy.

Mandarins and Ministers

Am I going doolally? Sitting quietly, reading the programme, waiting for the curtain to rise – as we still stay, although it now seldom actually does so, even if the theatre has one – another couple arrive with our seat numbers. Double booking? No, it's a matinee and our seats are for the evening. I am mortified. I, who as soon as I book anything on line – flights, trains, hotels, performances – immediately enter the details on the schedule in my commuter, file the e-confirmation, check the tickets when they arrive and again when transferring from file to wallet. I, who as Manager of Seaford Summer Theatre had so many double bookings on the last night of the 1956 season that I resorted to gradually nicking every dressing room chair to put in the aisles of the Clinton Hall. Today's house is technically full, but a cautions management has a couple of house seats in reserve. I was christened Francis D Reid – the D, ostensibly for David, was probably inserted against the Doollally likelihood of my advancing years.

But as soon as the curtain rises – or rather as the houselights fade down and the stagelights fade up (another quirk of theatre jargon) we are laughing – not just smiling – laughing with an occasional wipe of the eyes. To take such a television success as *Yes, Prime Minister* and transfer it to the stage without Paul Eddington and Nigel Hawthorne who became the most convincing Prime Minster and Cabinet Secretary in the history of British politics, is, as Sir Humphrey might well have put it, a courageous decision. As the play progresses, the improbability escalates in a series of situations and behavioural responses that would normally be classified as farce. But this is a play about politicians so we treat it as heightened reality. Our elected masters and their civil servants doubtless see themselves as actors in a world drama of the utmost seriousness; for better or for worse, we voters tend to regard them as comedians.

MAY 2011

Democratic unenlightened

It has been a wobbly week for Anglo-American democracy. A referendum has overwhelming rejected a change to our voting system that would more accurately reflect the wishes of the electorate. The Lib Dems have been so witch-hunted for their pragmatism by the very people who benefit from their restraint on the Tories that hopes of new era of consensus coalition government, as practised in the rest of Europe, has become a receding dream. And, across America, the killing of Osama bin Laden has triggered hysterical displays of vengeance worship. And to think that, as a teenager, I passionately believed that we were entering into a new age of enlightenment!

Baroque perfection

Occasionally, very occasionally, a performance reaches that ultimate perfection when there is not a single detail that could be even considered a possibility for improvement. I have never achieved this in my own work but there have been a few, a very few, occasions when I have enjoyed this ultimate experience as a member of the audience. Tonight is such a night. Trevor Pinnock and friends – harpsichord, flute, string quintet and soprano – visit the Norfolk & Norwich Festival to play Purcell, Bach and Handel in a perfectly structured programme. The fifth Brandenburg and second suite are framed by airs and dances from *The Fairy Queen* and a group of arias from *Semele* and *Alcina*. The timbre of the baroque flute is much fatter and rounder than its multi-keyed successors and Katy Bircher conjures up a particularly melting sound whether sustaining Bach's long melodic phrases or articulating his dances – the badinerie was stunning. Kate Royal sings as Katy Bircher plays – with a voice clean, smooth and rounded, she radiates a clear message that this is a wonderful aria that she is privileged to be singing. And what could I wish for more than Semele's *Endless Pleasure* and the *Tornami a vagheggiar* that featured in both my RSAMD graduation and 80th birthday party. On such a night, it is inevitable that an encore is demanded and we are given a stunning delivery of Cleopatra's *Da Tempeste*. Pinnock and friends really do get inside the music and share its bliss.

Mating dance

Guitars, castanets, tight trousers, stamping heels and flowing petticoats in abundance, but not a tambourine or mantilla in sight. Flamenco flirts with choreographic ideas from contemporary dance in two works – *Dualia*, an exploration of the gestures of relationships, and *La Leyenda*, a portrayal of the life of flamenco star Carmen Amaya – brought to Norwich by Ballet Nacional de Espana. The dancing is brilliant, the music pulsating, the energy infectious, and the sexual tension palpable – this is the mating game formalised and ritualised to an extreme.

Ballet Nacional de Espana in La Leyenda.

Period ambience

What better way to celebrate 300 years of the Unitarian Meeting House in Bury St Edmunds than a concert of trio sonatas by Handel and Telemann interspersed with sonatas for violin by Bach and for cello by Pieter Hellendaal – a Dutch pupil of Tartini who became pivotal to the 18th musical life of Kings Lynn and Cambridge. And if that were not enough to justify the inclusion of a rather engaging work in the programme, Hellendaal assisted Handel with a revival of *Acis & Galatea*. Tonight's musicians are the four ladies – recorder, violin, cello and harpsichord – of the Brook Street Band. Sitting in the front row we enjoy the close prominence of harpsichord, the biting texture of the gut strings and the pure fluting of the keyless recorder. And all in a superb early Georgian building with a similar footprint to the theatres of the period.

One of my yesterdays

Thirty years ago we were living in Bury St Edmunds where I was in the midst of what I consider to be the most important achievement of my professional life. Wilkins' 1819 Theatre Royal, having survived multiple ups and downs including 40 years as a brewery barrel store,

Model of the Theatre Royal Bury St Edmunds.

was locked into an accelerating spiral of decline and I turned it round. Just a couple of years in my theatric life but the ones I am most proud of. Mission accomplished, I returned to the world of making shows rather than selling them. The Theatre Royal has thrived ever since and is now beautifully restored to as close to its 1819 opening as indicated by current research tempered with current safety and comfort considerations. And it is thriving although, like all arts during the current cycle of cuts, the future holds less security than an enlightened society would wish. So today we walk around the town, sit in the Abbey Gardens, lunch in the Dog & Partridge and generally wallow in one, a very important one, of our yesterdays.

Flying circus grounded

Bury Theatre Royal lacks a fly tower and its grid does not support flying machines. So Monteverdi's muse remains an earthbound juggler without at all compromising *Monteverdi's Flying Circus*, a very enjoyable play about the great Venetian composer interspersed with the best tunes from his *Popea*, *Orfeo* and *Ulisse*. Anthony Pedley as Monteverdi gives what can only be described as a magnificent performance and, accompanied by two violins, two violas, cello, lute, harpsichord and percussion, the singers make lots of melting sound that is enhanced by the acoustic intimacy of the theatre. The final duet from *Poppea* is always ravishing and is particularly so tonight. An evening of sincerity without a hint of Monty Python.

JUNE 2011

Göttingen

Booking late, the only seat available is at the side of the second balcony where even the front row (the only row) has a severely restricted view of the stage of the venerable Deutsches Theater where the Handel renaissance began in 1920.

Teseo at Deutsches Theater Göttingen.

But the sound is magnificent, particularly from a good all round cast and a Festival Orchestra drawn from the cream of Europe's baroque players. Teseo is the final production of Nicholas McGegan's 21 year tenure as director of the Göttingen Handel Festival. There is an unusually large screen for the surtitles and as the houselights dim we see McGegan taking a call on his mobile, looking at his watch, and running into the theatre, his way barred by officious usherettes, taking the wrong staircase but eventually reaching the door to the stalls when the video cuts and our laughter switches to rapturous applause while he arrives in the pit to start the overture. The screen reverts to its normal purpose of translating the Italian libretto into German but occasionally shows as backstage moments and facebook entries in a sort of neo-brechtian gesture towards emphasising theatricality. Although there is no need for such video clips, they are unobtrusive and if they make the director happy while otherwise conforming to the period informed Göttingen production style, so be it. Sets are mostly cloths and wings with a couple of chandeliers in all scenes, day and night, costumes lavishly baroque and gestures historically histrionic. The New York Baroque Dance Company are choreographed in accord with period prints and choreographic diagrams. McGegan caresses the music lovingly and the result is delicious.

Matinees

Dillie Keane's polemic in *The Stage* against matinees provokes an outburst of correspondence to which I contribute.

Sorry Dillie, but as an octogenarian who may be somewhat spavined but does not consider himself a deadbeat, I enjoy matinees. Indeed they have become my favourite performance time to the extent that I never consider an evening show if a matinee is available. Why? Well, like many oldies, I tend to be quite lively at the beginning of the day but become increasingly frayed towards evening and, with a pension that reflects a lifetime of fees that amount to subsidising the arts, I can more easily afford the cheap afternoon seats offered by such enlightened theatres as we have in Norwich. In my experience we are not a "lot of old codgers nodding off in the stalls" but appreciative attentive discerning theatrelovers who behave with a deal more decorum than is often to be found in the evening. To suggest that matinees are performances when "a dispirited cast trudge through a comedy in utter silence" is an insult to our industry's professionalism to which I take umbrage as a life member of Equity.

Back in Halle

Last year I had to abort my 11th visit to the Halle Handel-Festspiele and return my tickets … a little matter of cardiac maintenance. But here I am once again in Handel's birthplace for that postponed tenth visit. And one again at the height of the *spargelsaison* where melting but delicately al dente sticks of white asparagus as long as a wide dinner plate are de rigeur.

Viva Vivica

Billed as star *sopranisten in a gala concert*, Vivica Genaux sings Handel, Hasse and Vivaldi with a glorious voice that fully justifies every single letter of *star* and *gala*. And she does it with such charm that we take her to our hearts and beg for encores which she is delighted to offer. Concerto Köln give delightfully dangerous but delightfully successful readings of the water music and a concerto grosso. Throughout the evening their principal oboist, Bendit Laurent, whether in the Handel, a Vivaldi Concerto or the obbligato to a Hasse aria that was really a duet for oboe and soprano, played with stunning technique and musicianship. Well worth coming to Halle for – and this is only day one.

Café Handel

Another ace soprano. Roberta Invernizzi explores two of Handel's anguished ladies – the abandoned Armida and the death contemplating Agrippina. I am not alone in finding a tendency for Handel's women to be more interesting than his men and in these early examples from his Italian tour, he leaves not a shred of passion untattered. Signora Invernezzi obliges with superbly vocalised grief supported by the two violins, cello, lute and harpsichord of Café Zimmerman who take their name from the coffee house music life of baroque Leipzig. With cantatas framed by sonatas, what better way to spend a hot Sunday morning than in the cool Löwengebäaude hall of Martin Luther University.

More Handel Women

Ottone may be king of Germania but this is really an opera about the women who impinge on his life, including a fine portrait of a pushy mum. With my slender homework unsupported by the German surtitles, my little brain is soon overtaken by the details of a plot that is a jungle of mistaken identities and misunderstandings. So I settle for a basic who's who, surrender to the music and enjoy the fairytale picture book sets revolving inside a wraparound cyclorama – although leaving the theatre with a suspicion that, once again, a director's lack of faith in the depth of Handel's empathy with the complexities of his characters, had given us camp when we, and Handel, deserved sincerity.

Händel Haus

Any visit to Halle has to include a pilgrimage to the house where he was born and lived his first 18 years. Over the years that I have been coming to Halle, it has been gradually but rigorously restored and the quality of the displays has matured. No visit is complete without a drink in the shade of the tree in the courtyard.

Handel Haus in Halle.

Opera Marionettistica

The credible staging of operatic battles is tricky and tonight's solution is to let the actors just sing and leave the acting to puppets. So the Italian Compagnia Marionettistica Carlo Colla e Figli are on the stage of the Goethe Theater in Bad Lauchstadt, the singers are in the side galleries and the Lautten Compagney are in the pit. The benefits are not just in the battle scenes – although this is the first time I have been convinced by the size of the Crusader army laying siege to Jerusalem in Handel's *Rinaldo* – but in the general scenic demands of baroque opera. This was Handel's first opera in London and, setting out to dazzle, gave him his

Rinaldo by Compagnia Marionettistica Carlo Colla e Figli, Goethe Theater Bad Lauchstadt.

biggest hit and became the most performed in his lifetime. Chariots drawn by two and three headed demons are no problem for marionettes while such magic as vanishing palaces and storm tossed seas is easily achieved. Handel's wonderful writing for the birds in the garden scene is beautifully realised both musically and scenically. Indeed the orchestra are magnificent throughout with Wolfgang Katschner getting to the heart of a score dazzling in its use of recorders, oboes, bassoon, four trumpets and baroque percussion timbres that I have never before heard but totally accept. The singers, free from the gymnastics of a director's conceptual fancies, get on with singing superbly. This is a night for superlatives and I have no hesitation in using them. Nine singers, 14 puppeteers, 25 musicians in a 450 seat theatre – this is the stuff of festivals.

A fine pair of organs

A gentle stroll around sun drenched Halle, cooling off with a *Flip Campari* (orange juice and Campari laced with vanilla ice cream) in the shade of the Handel memorial statue before a noon organ recital in the

Marktkirche where he was baptised. Handel is played on the Reichel (on which Handel learned to play) at the east end and Bach on the Schuke at the west.

Music for an occasion

Back at the Marktkirche for an evening performance of the *Occasional Oratorio*, a general purpose work suitable for any occasion requiring a triumphant restatement about the power and the glory of the almighty coupled with a stern warning about the consequences of sin. Solid Old Testament stuff underlined with resounding choruses accompanied by trumpets and drums giving it their full con belto with an intensity that could not possibly be sustained for anything approaching three hours. So Handel paces his oratorio with contemplative arias assuring us of the good life enjoyed by fearing God and abstaining from sin. Supported by the continuo and strings of the English Concert, soprano Julia Doyle makes a convincing case for placing our faith in the Lord, even if his mercy does seem to be conditional upon a somewhat draconian pursuit of vengeance. Church facilities inevitably place some strain upon us old codgers kept alive by diuretics: the Marktkirche has but one unisex toilet and the queue is so long that I miss my customary interval sekt. Whether this gains me an Old Testament brownie point I know not – however our knowledge of Handel suggests that such abstention was not his customary wont.

Elegant magic

This is the *Orlando* I have been waiting for. Nicola Humpel's production, resisting conceptual meddling, treats the opera as an elegant tale of confused and misunderstanding lovers eventually brought to a happy conclusion by the pivotal magician, Zoroastro. Supported by a pair of silent animateurs. Eschewing tricks and wands, there is a tingle of magic in the air. This atmosphere is created by a smooth, gentle acting style and simple scenic elements on a revolve backed by projections that are always apt and never mere graffiti. The evening is brimful of visual ideas – nothing superimposed, everything organic – growing naturally out of the seductive phrasing that Bernhard Forck draws from the period orchestra. Beautifully sung, acted with sincerity and lovingly played, a wonderful climax to a superb week of Handel.

Orlando at Opernhaus Halle.

Musical farce

Heading for the Kings' Head, a phone call alerts me to cancellation of tonight's performance of *The Barber of Salisbury* (aka *Seville*), so I divert to the TKSTS booth in Leicester Square and pick up a discounted centre stall for *Lend Me a Tenor* at the Gielguid (the Globe of my prime). I never got around to seeing the play 25 years ago but musical seems the natural genre for a 1930s tale of mistaken identities in a Midwest Grand Opera House where, for reasons too complex to summarise, three Otellos and six doors interact in every possible farcical permutation. The music is a pastiche of every operatic style except baroque while the dancing and choreography evoke – with tongue firmly in cheek – the Hollywood-Broadway musicals of my youth. A fun evening although I am surprised by the standing ovation.

A Midsummer days dream

For theatre technicians, the midsummer daydream is acquiring the goodies on display at the annual ABBT Show for their tool box. I am past such aspiration so I just admire the latest wizardry and select items for my retrospective wish list. I doubt if my lighting would have been any better but it would certainly have been easier – an opinion shared by the old colleagues I meet up with and reminisce as I wander from stand to stand.

Syncopated Monteverdi
Better operatic luck tonight in Islington where Mark Ravenhill directs his new translation of *The Coronation of Poppea* in an Opera Up Close production at the King's Head. Set on a thrust stage in a 200 seat room, the action is so up close that we audience are inescapably involved as plebs in the moral decline of a Roman hierarchy that, despite costumes probably sourced from Primark or Matalan, could be anywhere and anywhen. Decadence is everywhere but Monteverdi allows everyone involved to express their emotions with a musical sincerity that, especially in the more erotic moments, is non-judgemental about their motives. Seneca is the only character untainted by decadence and when, on Nero's orders, he commits suicide we are spared no details of his slow noble death, staining a pool of water that becomes so symbolical of the ethical disintegration that everyone becomes ankle deep in his blood. The King's Head may be London's smallest opera house but, despite this plus constraints imposed by the workload of the almost universally abandoned (but in my view desirable) repertoire system, the singing and acting is of a standard that cocks a snoot at the grander institutions. Being indicative rather than definitive, Monteverdi's score is open to wide interpretation. Alex Silverman has opted for piano, saxophone and double bass. The sax handles the sex well and with the bass, develops the syncopation which is dormant in much of the staccato repeating syllables of 17th century Venetian music. The final duet is, as always, ravishing.

Celebrating Mackerras
Beethoven, Britten, Handel, Janáček, Mozart, Puccini, Strauss, Sullivan and Verdi, join three conductors, two dozen soloists, chorus and orchestra of English National Opera for a Sunday night celebration of Sir Charles Mackerras. From the *Figaro* overture to the *Falstaff* final, it is an evening of happy memories in the opera house, concert hall, radio and gramophone. The jewel is the *La Réjouissance* from Handel's Fireworks played by the ENO wind and percussion augmented by 23 oboes, eight

bassoons, three contra bassoons, nine horns, eight trumpets and four drums from the Royal Academy. A truly joyously impressive sound! I worked with Mackerras only in my early days – and his – at Aldeburgh and Wexford, but I have been continuously pleasured ever since, particularly by his Mozart and Handel. My contemporaries are fading away.

Charles Mckerras.

Glyndebourne rehearsal

Next morning brings a further reminder of the inexorable progress of life's fade. Sitting in on rehearsals for *Rinaldo*, I realise that George and Mary Christie are the only contemporaries from my Glyndebourne decade (the 60s) still active there. Even the longest serving member of the production team, Keith Benson, joined a couple of years after I left. Sitting in the circle looking to the stage across a sea of production desks, one for each of the team that brings an opera to life – director and assistant, designer, lighting designer, lighting manger, projection designer, wardrobe and repetiteurs – do I feel nostalgia? Well, just a little bit. But, like so many past pleasures in life, perhaps cosier to recall than it would be to relive. And one of the memories is having to concentrate on balancing the light when I would much rather have just surrendered to the music. Moreover, it is a considerable pleasure to sit back and watch creative people working. The sound of the Orchestra of the Age of Enlightenment is ravishing in the timber warmth of the new Glyndebourne, and Ottavivo Dantone demonstrates how much the Italians, who came late to the rediscovery of period playing, are bringing to the glories of Handel.

Robert Carsen's production treats the opera as a school project in which teachers and pupils, investigate "Were the first crusaders inspired by religious idealism or political revenge" by assuming the roles and experimenting with the magic effects that contributed to making this the big hit that launched Handel's operatic career in London. In a particularly strong cast, Almirena, one of Handel's great women, is played magnificently by Sonia Prina

JULY 2011

Octagon
In the appropriate ambience of Thomas Ivory's 1756 Octagon Chapel in Norwich, the Bach Players investigate the influence of French music on the English composers of the restoration theatre. So we have arias and suites from Purcell and his contemporaries intermingled with those from Lully and his. This was a transitory period when the large range of string options of viols was settling into the string ensemble that would become standardised towards the end of the barque period and remain so until today. So the ensemble the haute contre violin and the tenore viola when appropriate. A fascinating and rewarding evening of music and architecture.

Kayleigh
With much grandparental pride, Jo and I go to the Islington Design Centre for the Young Designers' exhibition where granddaughter Kayleigh is exhibiting work that formed the centrepiece of her recent art school graduation show. Let her explain...

> My concern is to make jewellery that is both eco-friendly and personal to the wearer. The pieces are made from pulp of fibrous recycled paper and materials taken from the landscape – grass, berries, spices and flowers. These are all combined and placed in a mould in order to form the piece of jewellery. Each piece can be unique to the wearer, using a place, walk, a track – a location special to them. The design is developed from the map of the site, the physical features of the land carved into the plaster. This is used as the mould for the paper pulp which includes the flora of the place. At the end of its life, when the wearer is finished with it, the bracelet can be returned to its source: to sink back into the ground without harm.
>
> Fashion has become 'Fast' and time is not taken to consider the effect on the environment. My concept shows that jewellery does not have to be

made in this way, and that the fashion industry can make things more ethical.

These particular bracelets show the connection between generations. A lot has changed between now and the austerity of both World Wars. The 'Make do and Mend' slogan has had a big influence on my work. I want to bring this into the modern day world with a new and innovative technique.

The generation connection link is demonstrated by a photo of bracelets juxtaposed on her arms and her grandmother's. However her career ambitions are focused rather more towards backstage at the theatre rather than at the jewellers.

Kayleigh and Jo wearing Eco-friendly bracelets.

Carriage living

We are in the highlands, holidaying on the shores of Loch Awe in a railway carriage, vintage 1955. We are on the last remaining bit of track of Pier Sidings [our address] between Loch Awe station and pier. After a lifetime's daily shuffling between London and Edinburgh, our carriage was retired to Loch Awe as a tearoom but is now superbly restored, keeping all original features except where they would interfere with an all mod con lifestyle – microwave, satellite TV, shower, CD/DVD player and beds offering a five star sleep. The dining compartment is exactly as was and the original seats – properly sprung unlike today's ergonomic designs – are retained at each end of the saloon. The

Loch Awe railway carriage.

communication cord is in place as are such classic notices as *all tickets ready, shunt with care*, etc. A bookcase is filled with railway history and the corridor is decorated with old handbills. Loch Awe is on the single track West Highland Railway from Glasgow to Oban and there are three trains in each direction daily. In conjunction with sun and moon, they soon supersede clock and watch as the timepiece for our inactive response to a continuously changed landscape of loch, mountains and sky that gives our static carriage an illusion of movement. A week of bliss.

AUGUST 2011

Exam solstice

Shrieks, gasps, tears of joy and stiff upper lips are upon us on once again. The release of exam results – first A levels and then GCSE – has usurped the status once reserved for lambing and the harvest. So two August Thursdays mark a solstice when we can depend on the media to show us the envelopes being opened, inform us that the results are better than ever this year and debate whether the exams have become easier. Acres of newsprint are devoted to league tables that have little relevance to education and encourage even further obsession with easily measurable instant outcomes. Exams, in one form or another, are necessary to assess attainment but what may be appropriate for objectively measurable areas such as language, maths and science can be over simplistic for subjective areas such as literature and the arts which, being further disadvantaged by the pursuit of instant outcomes, are becoming marginalised. Essential life skills are mostly based on logic (and therefore measurable) but many of the decisions to be made in a caring, democratic society come from an instinct that has been honed by ideas and concepts that are absorbed and gradually processed through mind and soul to become an intrinsic part of a rounded individual.

Riots

For several months, watching television reports of violence erupt all over the Middle East, we have consoled ourselves with the belief that looting and rioting neither could nor would happen here. Wrong! It could and this weekend it has. Libya and Syria have relinquished their headline coverage in favour of Croydon, Tottenham, Manchester – and even Ealing. Awestruck, we have watched shops looted and scorched while rescue attempts by individuals and the emergency services are met with sickening violence. The iconic image is a bleeding youth being ostensibly helped while the contents of his backpack are stolen. The police are caught so off-guard that, for the first night they join the rest of us in just dropped-jaw watching. Government minsters abort their holidays and fly home for an emergency session of parliament. The full force of the law swings into action, CCTV footage is analysed, courts sit all night and custodial sentences for nicking doughnuts lead to a prison overfill crisis. The rioting is not racist: Mr Patel suffers the same fate as Starbucks. Biblically, it could be labelled an outbreak of original sin but it seems to be more of a spontaneous letting off of steam led by the growing underclass in our classless society. Will we tackle such root causes as housing, unemployment and education? Or just be content with vengeance.

Heart Emergency
Not mine but Jo's. Classic breathing and tight chest symptoms. I ring the out-of-hours doctor and a paramedic arrives within minutes with oxygen and a portable EGC, closely followed by an ambulance crew who whisk us off to A&E. A troponin blood test confirms heart attack and two days later an angiogram explores the extent of the vascular damage. I am comforted that she is in the care of my cardiologist. Jo and I are good at sharing.

Jo home
That was on Sunday. The family moved rapidly and smoothly into support mode and today she is home with a complex medication cue sheet. I have rather enjoyed my kitchen takeover.

Edinburgh Nichtnachtmusic
Overnighting in Edinburgh during the last days of the Festival – the International one, the Fringe finished last week – I find that there is nothing, yeah nothing, that I want to see tonight. Or to hear. Oh, dear!

SEPTEMBER 2011

Elite but not Elitist

It is the first of September and I am in Glasgow for a transformation scene. Today the Royal Scottish Academy of Music and Drama becomes the Royal Conservatoire of Scotland. Why? What's the difference? Well, in short, a university offers theoretical studies supported by performing whereas a conservatoire emphasises performing supported by theory. Both approaches – learning about how it is done or learning to do it – are valid but, at a time when we are debating options for backstage training and rediscovering the value of apprenticeships, it is a distinction worth considering. There has been a conservatoire approach to performer education in Scotland since the 1847 founding of an institution that has undergone several name changes to meet the expansion of its size and scope. With degree programmes now including not just music, drama and production skills but dance, film, video and crossovers between all these areas, any attempt at an omnibus title would result in a tongue-twister reducing to a meaningless logo, so yet another change has become inevitable. *Conservatoire* says it all – so this is surely the final name change. The Scots have always led the way in education and their Conservatoire is no exception. A launch video on the theme 'we are' indicates the extent of RCS activities. It ends with a wonderful phrase We are *Elite but not Elitist*.

Bucking the trend

The world may be in economic meltdown, but in the midst of what is clearly a recession in all but definition, PLASA is bigger, brighter and louder than ever. Or so it seems as I hasten through the displays of LEDs, wigglies, smoke generators, artless projections, gramophones and everything needed to upstage the performer – every tool in the kit microprocessed into submission.

Afternoon Theatre

Some weeks ago Dillie Keane's column in *The Stage* referred to matinees as a "dispirited cast trudging through a comedy in utter silence" watched by a "lot of old codgers nodding off in the stalls". This triggered some lively correspondence, including my suggesting that her comments were "an insult to our industry's professionalism to which I take umbrage as a life member of Equity". This afternoon I join a full house of sprightly old codgers laughing non-stop at Alan Ayckbourn's comedy *Season's Greetings*. Ayckbourn characters abound in human frailties that we all recognise in others but rarely in ourselves, and the family that he gathers for a dysfunctional Christmas are a gloriously mismatched collection of the people we meet daily – exaggerated to the threshold of caricature perhaps but with such fine tuning as never to go beyond reality. Oh Silly Dillie – you are a truly Ackbourn character!

A virtuoso George III

Leading one of the largest tourist casts in recent years (other than the RSC or RNT), David Haig's virtuoso George III ensures another splendid afternoon for a full house of us old codgers. Lots of laughter but moments of deeply concerned sadness, including a moist-eyed first act curtain, as the King's doctors try bizarre cures

David Haig as King George III.

for misdiagnosed madness. It was probably porphyria with the cure spontaneous and occurring despite the horrific treatments prescribed. Alan Bennett's exploration of 18th century medicine and politics is masterly. Today's doctors may have magnificent diagnostic aids and truly magical potions at their disposals but the politicians? The only change seems to be their clothes.

Romantic come lately

After a lifetime poised between early baroque and late classicism, I am finally absorbing romanticism. Teenage exposure to Carl Rosa *Boheme* and *Butterfly* led to dismissal of Puccini as gushing verismo. Six months touring as the organ grinder (non-singing) gave me some affection for the little one-acter *Il Tabarro* and I took advantage of the opportunities offered by Michel Redgrave's production of *La Boheme* in Henry Bardon's designs to do one of my best lighting designs for Glyndebourne. That was 45 years ago – 45 years during which I have studiously avoided

Puccini until tonight when taking a punt on a DVD of Franco Zeffirelli's Met *Boheme*, the verismo penny dropped.

OCTOBER 2011

Miller's Passion

The division of music drama into opera and oratorio is rather artificial – a matter of convenience. The oratorio allowed subjects once considered too sensitive for the stage on biblical or secular grounds to be presented without scenery, costumes or movement – or, rather more mundanely, without opera's notorious resource hunger. But many oratorios have a much tighter dramatic structure than the average opera. None more so than Bach's *St Matthew Passion*. From the moment some years ago when I saw a telecast, Jonathan Miller's staging has been a must on my wish list. Although his first choice was the Roundhouse, his production works very well in the National Theatre's Olivier.

Three seating rows at the back of the stage give an arena feeling which is enhanced by the orchestra formation of twin arcs, one up and one downstage of a raised platform. These arcs do not quite join to form

Jonathan Miller's Bach St Mathew Passion.

an ellipse, leaving gaps for the soloists and chorus to come, go, and linger. The strings of the upstage orchestra are to prompt of a central chamber organ and the wind to OP, with a reversed disposition for the downstage orchestra. This symmetry complements Bach's musical formality. Streetwise casual is the dress code for singers and musicians who, when not singing or playing, are concerned onlookers. Obbligato players leave their desks during arias to interacting with their alter-ego singers. The evangelist, a rather detached commentator in the concert hall, becomes an involved narrator on the stage. Moving among the cast, whether narrating at the centre or observing at the periphery, he guides us through this familiar moment of history as if it were a new experience and happening now. Despite a lifetime familiarity with the story and its musical setting, I never fail to be moved by the arias and the chorus shriek of **Barabbas!** But tonight's staging brings even more poignancy and I move closer to an understanding of why Christianity has defied all its misinterpreters to last so long.

Spitfire largo

When I was lad, a tune called *Handel's largo* was played on solemn occasions. That was before rediscovery that the master of biblical oratorio was primarily a man of the theatre and that the tune was the aria *Ombra mai fu* sung by King Xerxes to a plane tree extolling is shady

English Touring Opera Xerxes.

virtues. And now tonight Wing Commander Xerxes sings it to the tail of his spitfire – the plane tree becomes an aeroplane in the English Touring Opera production of *Serse*. Forget ancient Persia. We are on a Battle of Britain airfield and the love pentangle involves pilots and nurses hindered by a comedy erk but abetted by a white coated boffin who is an amalgam of Spitfire designer R. J. Mitchell and dambuster Barnes Wallis. Previous updating experiences lead me to expect anachronisms but there are none of any consequence; the idea is so consistently followed through that Handel seems to be setting Nicholas Hytner's translation rather than the original libretto. With ETO moving from the Arts Theatre to the University Concert Hall for this Cambridge visit, I arrive in a trepidation mode that is increased with discovery that the orchestra are in a pit of Wagnerian depth so low that the only way they can take their curtain call is by waving their bows above the parapet. But the sound is lovely in row C.

The rise and fall of Expectations
The European financial crisis worsens daily. The politicians in their various "G" configurations meet with increasing frequency to come up with increasingly expensive but inadequate solutions. Alas, our aspirations have become expectations. And there is just not enough wealth to support these expectations. The differential between the haves and the have-nots that gradually shortened during much of the twentieth censure is widening. Banker bonuses and tycoon salaries are the universal target of envy and discontent. Extended life expectancy is a time bomb. Our expectations will have to revert aspirations.

NOVEMBER 2011
A slight yearning for Versailles
After a lifetime's uneasy flirtation with French baroque, I now feel comfortable with its musical idiom to an extent bordering on addiction. English National Opera's *Castor et Pollux* is an evening of gorgeous sounds. The flutes and trumpet are keyless baroque but Christopher Curnyn draws excellent period-informed playing from the modern strings, oboes, and bassoons of the resident band. With the musicians raised to floor level and every scenic surface, including the 'cloths', clad in untreated plywood, the sonority in mid-stalls is closer than normal for pre-romantic operas in the vast Coliseum auditorium. At a time when theatre assumes that contemporary relevance must be made so clear that audiences have no need to work it out for themselves, there is an inevitability that the staging is based on modern dress, violence, blood and an abundance of dangly bits. The singers rush hither and thither, throwing themselves against the wooden walls with such vigour as to cause amazement that they have any breath left to sing. But indeed they

have and the vocal quality, solo and ensemble, is uniformly high. Some of the directorial fancies, however, distract from the proceedings rather than enhance them. When the chorus ladies slowly drop their knickers to reveal another pair, then another pair, and so on until the floor is littered with piles of them, the triggered memory is pantomime dames preparing for bed. Once again a staging that, although not actually getting in the way of a great musical evening, fails to enhance it. From time to time it is difficult to suppress some yearning for the elegance of Versailles.

Backstage with Degas

I discovered Degas in 1952 and was smitten. The exhibition in the Royal Scottish Academy coincided with the Edinburgh Festival when I took to the stage as a silent extra with the Hamburg Opera. Visiting the exhibition while in thrall to the magical mystical world that I was discovering behind the curtain of the King's Theatre, I was enchanted by this backstage view of dancers at work. It was during that 1952 Festival that I resolved to attempt a life in the theatre. I knew the chances of

Picasso's backcloth for Le Train Bleu at Degas Exhibition.

survival were slim but nothing ventured, nothing gained. So the Royal Academy's **Degas and the Ballet – *Picturing Movement*** is one of the déjà vu moments that are a pleasure point of old age. The exhibition is full of old friends – paintings met in galleries across the years or familiar from books and postcards – now united in a clever juxtaposition. Perhaps the most exciting is the bronze of *Little dancer aged fourteen* at the centre of a round room with Degas' 20 sketches hung on the walls at viewpoints from which he drew them as he circled his model. His capture of movement in still images is masterly, whether the sequential drawings of limbs or the capture of en pointe so precise that we just know she is moving because otherwise she would topple. Degas was painting at a time of early experiments with photographic animation and the exhibition explores these techniques and his response. A truly wonderful display of ballet and the artist's working process in the era centred on the 90s.

Adaptability revisited

The ABTT could not have been given a better kickstart than the 1961 international conference on *Planning Adaptable Theatres* mounted only a few months after the inauguration of the Association. So it is appropriate that the events to celebrate the ABTT golden jubilee should include a discussion on *Do Adaptable Theatres Work?* led by a panel of architects, consultants and users with experience of flexible theatre formats. As one of the few survivors of the 1961 conference, I am invited to attempt a summing up at the end, comparing the sort of issues raised 50 years apart – in so far as it is possible to compare an evening debate with one of five days.

There is a strong resonance between the problems identified then and now but tonight's debate is gentler, more reasoned and informed by intervening experience. Back then a lot of us were young revolutionaries with fire in our bellies – firebrands like Peter Hall, Stephen Joseph, Disley Jones, Sean Kenny, Richard Pilbrow, David Collison, Ian Albery, Rod Ham and, yes, Francis Reid were barely into their thirties. Cries of "Down with the Proscenium" came from a group so vocal that they seemed intent on manning the barricades in defence of their cause. This was tempered by such older but still passionate warriors as Michel St Denis, Richard Southern, Norman Marshall, Percy Corry and Fred Bentham. The conference included papers and comments from Canada, France, Germany, India, South African and USA. Many of the projects discussed in 1961 were on the drawing board whereas we now have lots of adaptable theatres and every theatre is now expected to include some considerable degree of flexibility. The problems remain but experiment has produced some of the solutions. Are the upcoming generation passionate or complacent? I don't know. Unlike 1961, they were not present tonight.

Birthday reprised

Invited to Dinner with Handel, I am somewhat surprised to find that Norwich Theatre Royal and Glyndebourne have got together to celebrate my 80th. Many old friends and some new, although I am not quite sure whether Glyndebourne's Chairman, Gus Christie, counts as old or new – I last met him as a toddler visiting the production desk with his grandfather. In response to the toast I recall how the Theatre Royal has been an ongoing thread in my life since Glyndebourne. Apart from enjoying many happy lighting experiences, Angus had his first job there and the girls worked in the box office. Moreover, the auditorium contains my monument to posterity: the lighting bridge that I specified in 1968 remains, despite all efforts to remove it by a series of architects and consultants whose wishes have been consistently foiled by an alliance of lighting designers and structural engineers. The production is the *Rinaldo* that I sat-in on June rehearsals for at Glyndebourne (p.45). Tonight's singers and orchestra may be less starry but singing, playing and ensemble are of a standard that would grace any operatic stage anywhere. Getting into the taxi afterwards, the driver says "Enjoy opera?", pushes a button and we have Verdi all the way home.

Don Pasquale with a twist

Glyndebourne have also brought *Don Pasquale* with them – a new production not yet in their summer festival. It is an opera I know well from seeing many performances and six months of stage managing it for Opera for All, lighting it for Phoenix Opera and at Wexford. So every note, every orchestral texture, has a familiarity to wallow in. And I do. Singers who can act, musicians with uninhibited confidence, designs that keep the pace by revolving from one room to another and a directors who trusts her composer, librettist and audience enough to give them the story as written – backdating from 19th to 18th century rather than trying to find contemporary relevance and hammer it home. Until the last bar when, picking up a hint dropped in the first act, Malatesta rather than Ernesto gets Norina. I have often thought that the soprano would be better off with the clever baritone than with the wimpish tenor. Tonight she does and I am pretty sure Donizetti would approve.

Granpa's footsteps?

Kayleigh is working a follow spot at Ipswich Wolsey. Has she caught grandpa's theatre bug? What better basis for diagnosis than 70 panto performances in seven weeks? Her plotting, unlike her grandfather's, is certainly a model of clarity – and entertainingly decorative.

DECEMBER 2011

Handel well (cyber) Met

While there is nothing quite like the contact – ears and eyes – of a live performance, high definition digital relays have introduced a serious alternative. Although there are losses, there are considerable benefits. Cinemas, especially the smaller 'art' cinemas, are more comfortable than most opera houses, the sightlines are clearer and the camera can introduce a considerable degree of intimacy into a cavernous auditorium. This is a particular advantage for baroque opera – although we are inevitably at the mercy of the director's sensitivity in selecting close-ups. And crucially, when you live in Norwich and your nearest opera house is in Amsterdam, it is nice to be able to just pop up the road for a Sunday afternoon at the Cybermet … particularly for a Rodelinda with the likes of Renée Fleming, Andreas Scholl and Iestyn Davies in period frocks, proper scenery and no desire to hammer home contemporary relevance. Uniformly great singing and an orchestral sound that made up in richness for the inevitable lack of period instrument articulacy.

Christmas crisps

The ABTT ends its golden anniversary year in a blaze of austerity. Arriving at 1pm for the annual Christmas get together amid the splendours of the salon at Drury Lane, anticipating the usual rather good buffet, we find neither chilli nor rice nor salad well tossed. Just plates of crisps. The official line is the late discovery of the suspension of the Lane's catering operation due to the audience demographic for Shrek. As a phone call to Marks & Spencer would have produced party platters at very short notice, one can only suspect that the ABTT and its sponsors are feeling the economic pinch. Fortunately the wine flowed as freely as the conversation. As I left for a late pub lunch, I could not help feeling that an anniversary year that seldom roared has gone out like a lamb.

Christmas lights

The ALD ends its golden anniversary year with a five hour lunch of traditionally trimmed turkey. Presenting the inscribed mounted stencil that certifies the award of an ALD Fellowship on the occasion of Rick

Fisher's stepping down after 15 years as chairman, I note that while the chalice he inherited had been quite drinkable, the one he was passing on was full of frizzante.

For unto us

Throughout the 19th and well into the 20th centuries, Handel was regarded as a man of the church. But, although he wrote oratorios on biblical themes, we now recognise that essentially he

Presenting Rick Fisher with Fellowship of ALD.

was a man of the theatre. While *Messiah* ensured his immortality, its success overshadowed his works for the stage. Like all his oratorios, it is a highly dramatic work despite being written for performance in concert rather than with all the trappings of the operatic stage. I have been particularly moved by stagings of *Belshazzar, Brockes Passion, Hercules, Israel in Egypt, Jeptha, Samson, Saul, Solomon, Theodoa* – and *Messiah*. Although his Christian commitment is in no doubt, his music is equally applied to a universal uplift, both the sacred and secular. The early soprano duet *No, di voi non vo'fidarmi* ('No, I do not trust you two, blind love, cruel beauty' becomes the sublime *Messiah* chorus *For unto us a child is born* that crystallises Christmas. Tonight's performance is on the stage – but not staged although set within tastefully glittered panto portals – of Norwich Royal. All the tempi are just and a super cast is led by Iestyn Davies (magnificent in *O thou that tellest good tidings to Zion*). The ambience and the seats beat most Gothic architecture, whether spiritual or secular.

A Christmas question

The seasonal backstage quiz in *The Stage* asks is *Carry on Fading* (a) A guide to dyeing for costume makers? (b) An account of the career of Kenneth Williams? (c) A memoir by Francis Reid?

Christmas past

Thirty Christmas eves ago I completed my tenure of the Theatre Royal in Bury St Edmunds. It was the first night (4pm) of the panto with the Friends of the Theatre offering mulled wine with mince pies in the interval and the Operatic Society singing carols in the street as the audience left the theatre. A final drink with the staff before they pushed me out the door with a shout of *Cue Sunset!* Turning the Bury theatre around was the pinnacle of my professional life. And at anniversary moments like today, I allow myself a brief glow of pride.

Handling Handel

No risk getting the turkey out of the oven – my Christmas present from Santa (Jo) Claus is magnificent oven gloves for when it's too hot to Handel.

Hogmanay

(28) Too hot to handle.

It has perhaps not been the easiest of years. But despite a heart attack and nine months bandaged from knee to toe, Jo has been her usual cheerful resilient self. And in a year when arthritis has crept from my knees into my hands, the theatre world has astonished my by celebrating my octo-survival. Much pleasure has been provided by operas, plays, concerts, books, theatres, CDs, DVDs and TV. Children and grandchildren are successful and happy. We could legitimately be described as a happy and loving family. So, although it may not have been the easiest of years, it has been a good one. I am content. But my contentment is tainted with guilt at my cosy oasis in a world overflowing with the miserable consequences of rampant intolerance and greed.

JANUARY 2012

How Mony?

As Mons Meg, the giant cannon given to James II of Scotland in 1457, announces the New Year on television, Jo and I raise our glasses of Glenfiddich to wish each other a Happy New Year for the 55th time. Ten minutes later, after a reel from Andy Bain and Phil Cunningham, we are off to bed. As I heave myself up the stairs with the help of both handrails, I find myself singing

> *A guid new year to ane an' a'*
> *An' mony may ye see*
> *An' during a' the years to come*
> *O happy may ye be*

as a montage of old years seen out and new years seen in escapes momentarily from rusty memory cells. Mony I did see … but … just how mony may I yet see? Well, happy I intend to be during a' the years to come.

New Year happiness
My new year is turning out to be rather happier than expected. Arthritis slowly advanced through my limbs during advent until my finger joints were so painfully stiff that eating the turkey became an exercise in dysfunctional dexterity. Having checked cures on the internet and finding only gloom, I visit my GP seeking help in hope rather than in certainty but the prescribed Naproxen turns out to be a miracle pill worthy of an opera libretto.

Hearing the light backwards
My habitual first acquaintance with any illustrated book has long been to flick through from the back. But the latest edition of *Hearing the Light* is designed to be read this way. It begins at the back and the index is at the front. It is a Japanese translation.

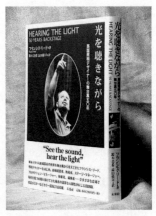
Japanese edition of Hearing the Light.

Cleopatra
The plots of Handel's plots are not easy to follow but Tim Albery's production is probably just about the clearest exposition I have encountered of not just *Guilio Cesare in Egito* but quite possibly any baroque opera. Hints of pyramids embellished with the stark greys of Rome and the sensuous golds of Egypt rotate within masking topped with the recurrent lettering SPQR

(*Senatus Populusque Romanus*) of the Roman Empire. A setting that carries metaphoric resonances and responds to light to give an unfolding sequence of pictures to pleasure the eye, serve the action and support the music. Handel's women are more fascinatingly complex than his men and Cleopatra is one of his finest creations. Sarah Tynan captures the emotional turmoil of a young girl dealing with teenage emotions while driven to a hasty acquisition of cunning in order to thwart the regal ambitions of her narcissistic psychopathic brother. Cleopatras often verge on caricature but tonight's is a totally believable person whose anguish we share rather than merely observe. Cornelia, so often played as a simple misery guts, also becomes much more real and rounded person in Anne Taylor's hands. And, indeed this pursuit of credibility extends throughout an ensemble who act and sing to a standard that ensues Opera North a place at the top Handel Opera House table. The only small blot on a potentially perfect evening is the orchestral contribution: despite good individual playing and some felicitous ornamentation, there is too much tendency towards plodding accompaniment rather than crisp dialogue. Well worth the expedition – a seven hour round trip hours in ambling cross country trains to Leeds.

Enchanting pastiche

Shipwreck the pairs of lovers from *Midsummer Night's Dream* on Prospero's *Tempest* island and give them lots of Handel and some Vivaldi to sing, garnishing with Campra, Purcell and a masque danced to Rameau. Combining painted scenery with digital projection, hire Jeremy Sams and William Christie to concoct a new baroque opera for an elite cast of Handel singers. Just the recipe for an enchanted afternoon to be enjoyed in the comfort of Norwich Cinema City by courtesy of Met Opera HD Live.

Oh that there had been a librettist of Jeremy Sams calibre available to Handel. Unlike the average baroque opera plot, *The Enchanted Island* is crystal clear without any need for homework. Its English words, both recit and aria, are crisply to the point while in empathy with the changing emotions of the music. Vocal and acting opportunities abound for a cast who seize them to portray a series of people – real humans within baroque conventions of gesture and movement – supported by gorgeous costumes and a setting that respects period scenic conventions but absorbs today's technology. The combination of baroque wave machinery with gauze

Enchanted Island.

and video projection enables Ariel – Danielle de Niese, splendidly agile in limbs and voice – to invoke a truly magical sinking of the lovers and their ship. She enchants throughout and the inclusion of Vivaldi's *Agitata da due venti* from *Griselda* for her final aria in celebration of her freedom is masterly in choice and execution. Joyce di Donato is gloriously evil as the sorceress Sycorax pitting her wits against Propsero (David Daniels) but no match for Placido Domingo's Neptune whose first entry is set to the monumental *Zadok the Priest*. Confusion reigns for three hours but all ends happily. The beckmesser brigade nit-picked but I loved it.

Remembering rep

TV channel browsing chances upon the movie of *The Cat and the Canary*, the sixth play in the weekly rep season that kick started my life in theatre. Watching it triggers not a single memory although my programme files reveal that the characters in the film have the same names as those in the play. The screenplay, however, seems to use only the title, plot idea and characters. And I suspect that these have been rewritten – according to the programme I played Hendricks but have no memory of it being a part worthy of casting Edward Fox. My roles in Tonbridge Rep were rarely longer than one-liners of the quality and quantity of "I am the butler, here is your tea". But cuttings reveal that there was much more excitement than the play on the opening Monday of January 17th 1955. The News Chronicle

THE CAT AND THE CANARY
By JOHN WILLARD

MAMMY		VIVIENNE FIELD
ROGER CROSBY		CHARLES H. BOLT
HARRY BLYTHE		DONALD SARTAIN
SUSAN SILLSBY		ANNETTE ANDERSON
CECILEY YOUNG		COROL ATKINS
CHARLES WILDER		MAURICE NEVILLE
PAUL JONES		JACK BRADLEY
ANNABELLE WEST		VAL KINSEY
HENDRICKS		FRANCIS REID
DR. PATERSON		WILLIE LOYTER

Play produced by JACK BRADLEY

SYNOPSIS OF SCENES
The Library of Glencliffe Manor.

ACT I. Night
ACT. 2 A few minutes later
ACT. 3 A few minutes later

Stage Director—Francis Reid Stage Manager—Donald Sartain Scenery designed by Mark Tyme
Next Month—THE DOMINANT SEX

The Cat and the Canary at Tonbridge.

front page photo, captioned *The show must go on – even if the stalls are at least three feet deep in water*, while the Tunbridge Wells Advertiser pictured me and the director in our wellies carrying actresses through the flooded auditorium. Headlines in the national and local press would surely boost attendance we thought. Alas, audience numbers plummeted and it was several weeks before the fear of a damp house was overcome. I can recall the flood with clarity but any details of the play other than its title are as blank as blank can be.

FEBRUARY 2012

Early doors
The winter has been exceptionally mild but today it's a bit chilly around the early doors – as Aileen Vernon habitually said as she came through the stage door of Glasgow Alhambra on wintry days. I have never discovered whether this was an expression generally used by old pros or just by the redoubtable Aileen who taught me to stage manage panto. The doors in question are the gallery doors and the early refers to the higher price when they first opened to the queue for the unreserved bench seats. In my student days, the early doors of the Edinburgh Kings were 1/6 (7½p) but if the queue was short it was worth writing a further ten minutes until the price dropped to a shilling (5p).

Opera as was
The first snow of winter comes at last and we awake to look out on a deep and crisp and even that is worthy of Wenceslas. By evening the gritted

roads are clear but the pavements are lethal. We slither in and out of taxis to reach Ukraine Opera on tour with *La Traviata*. Cold out but cosy within – not just played in period and place but with acting and scenery that would have been familiar to Verdi. Reasonable voices and a good band. Violetta gives her all in the death scene – well over the top, but the music can take it – and as the curtain falls, Jo and I look at each other and say "Donald Wolfitt!".

Distant lighting

Invited to contribute an essay on lighting design for a proposed new Technical Stagecraft Compendium I reply:

Having given some detailed thought to this project, I have come to the conclusion that I am not the man for the job. It needs somebody younger – someone actively designing light. And there are lots of them about. My last lighting design was in 2001 and I taught my last class in 2007. At that point I resolved that I would only write/speak about lighting in a historical context.

Nevertheless, when I got your request I thought it might be fun to take on the challenge of trying yet again to find words to explain lighting design. But last night I came to the stark conclusion that the process of lighting design is so far in my past that I am no longer interested in it. Indeed when I go to the theatre nowadays, I only notice the lighting if it is excruciatingly bad or superbly good. It takes me barely five minutes to flick through L+SI before consigning it to the bin. I am still passionate about theatre but my interest in lighting now seems like a passing phase! Sorry!

Relieving the itch

Aches and itches come and go in us elderly. Currently my back has a transient itch. So when I sit I tend to rub against the back of the chair, muttering *God Bless the Duke of Argyle* in appreciative memory of his introduction of scratching posts as an amenity for his livestock.

Creative conversation

Not, as one might suppose, about the fiction that results from creative writing but a label for the conversations about creativity that the Royal Conservatoire of Scotland has with its honorary doctorates. So I find myself sitting on the stage of the Conservatoire's Athenaeum Theatre talking to three video cameras and an invited audience about some of the whys and wherefores of my life in the theatre

Dining with sponsors

Dining with Northern Light, sponsors of the conversation, on Scottish-Chinese cuisine with a hint of nouvelle, I spurn the black pudding spring rolls as a creative step too far. I am with friends from the golden (at least in retrospect) years of Howard & Wyndham so we exchange tales of Freddie, Cruiky, Rikki, Stanley, Stella, Jimmy, et al. As always, we remember the laughs rather than the tears.

Patronage

Stepping into pastures new is rather nice when you have reached the "well, that's it" years. Especially when it only requires attaching one's name to a new enterprise and smiling benignly upon it. Associating oneself with any enterprise is risky but the Edinburgh Lighting and Sound School is a new backstage training approach to be encouraged. In hotel terminology, it is having a 'soft opening' with five students towards a target ceiling of 15. At a time when higher education is driven by a bums on seats culture, such small numbers are to be welcome. As the core philosophy of the school is a series of placements with theatres, rental companies and event producers of all genre's from rock to conference, student numbers are limited by the number of opportunities available for meaningful experience at the coal face of production staging. After meeting with students and lunching with staff, I have no regrets that I gave the idea my blessing when it was but a dream of its founder, lighting designer George Tarbuck.

The tablet decade

While life expectancy has increased, the final decade is likely to be marked by illness and increasing pharmaceutical dependency. So sayeth the statisticians and my daily dosage of three diuretics, one statin, one aspirin, three inhalers and NSAIDs as required would certainly seem to tick their boxes. Without this chemical intervention I would probably be ill but with them I am reasonably hale and make a fair impression of being hearty. So have I gone beyond Shakespeare's seventh age? Am I perhaps at 8.2?

And then the medicines
Pills and potions, swallow and inhale
Before our food, and with it, or thereafter
For in our last decade (the statisticians say)
Thou shalt by chemicals postpone thy timely exit to Elysium
So man, and woman too, hath now not seven but eight ages
To strut or zimmer their brief hour upon this mortal stage.

Concrete

The only concrete theatre for which I have any enthusiasm is the Bädische Staastheater in Karlsruhe. Indeed affection has grown to an extent for which love would not be an exaggeration. Although not at all dismissive of the Aalto Theater in Essen, Karlsruhe is my favourite asymmetric auditorium – a format worthy of closer scrutiny by theatre

Hessisches Staastheater Karlrsruhe.

architects. Don't ask me why … if there is any logic, I am neither able to speculate nor feel any need to do so. But what is the logic for a symmetrical house apart from customary practice established by the Greeks? In Karlsruhe the fairface concrete, juxtaposed with marble and timber, really does present a fair face, mostly raw but tellingly paint washed where appropriate. Furthermore, every time I walk in – and this is my 12th Handel festival visit – I am immediately struck by its pristine maintenance

Neobaroque

Hearing *Dino und Die Arche* with an innocent ear, I would happily accept it as the rediscovered work of a forgotten baroque composer. But the music is by Thomas Leiniger, a 30-year-old who has not only mastered the style of Handel and his contemporaries but writes good tunes – an approach that is apt for an opera about Dinosaurs and Darwinism aimed at an audience age 6+. Darwinism may explain the extinction of the dinosaurs but creationism? Well they arrive too late at the Ark for check-in and are denied boarding. This is perhaps fortunate in view of their weight, although the operatic species – the six singing dinosaurs are splendid caricatures from the world of 18th century cartoon – are at risk as a result of their

Dino und Die Arche.

psychological rather than physical development. But Darwin was sad about all the lost species and the creationists like a happy audience so the dinosaurs become birds. A cast of 20 and orchestra of 35 in a 300 seat theatre with tickets €4 to €8.50.

Neocastrati

When I was rescued by music from teenage angst, countertenors were a rarity. There was only Alfred Deller plus a few chaps lurking incognito in cathedral choirs. Now they are aplenty. Tonight's *Der Vier Contertenore* has four, each giving us three arias interspersed with orchestral Handel – a couple of overtures and movements from the water music. Aware that their predecessors, the castrati, were the celebrity divas of the baroque stage, they deliver arias by Galuppi, Porpora, Vivaldi and Handel with such gusto that few passions are left unshredded in the tattering while the quality of the singing has the audience chorusing their bravos in a frenzy of applause. In addition to some of the great Handel show-pieces from *Alcina, Ariodante* and *Rinaldo* there are arias from the likes of Porpora and Vivaldi who specialised in providing the castrati with the vocal gymnastics in which they excelled. The orchestra, Collegium 1704 in excellent form, offering some delicately different interesting Czech perception of Handel that included embellishments of the water music to tickle the aural palette.

Chamber trumpet

Although, to quote Dryden, *the trumpet's loud clangour excites us to arms* – it is not a sound much associated with chamber music. But the natural trumpet also has a mellow capability that can blend with string quintet and harpsichord. In its higher registers, as an alternative to its customary strident assertions, it can sustain a dialogue with the violins and oboes in the ornamental flourishes of baroque allegri. All the ingredients for a Sunday morning concert by trumpet, string quintet and harpsichord.

Neodivas

Driven by a mix of politics and passion, Alexander the Great is torn between his affections for two sopranos throughout the four hours of Handel's *Alessandro*. That the two ladies were originally played by the 'rival queens', Bordoni and Cuzzoni, with the celebrated castrati heartthrob Senesino as Alexander must have added a considerable frisson to the 1726 première. The score is richly orchestrated and a large (36) period orchestra produce ravishing sounds. Festival standards of singing, acting and costuming but a scenic environment offered little support.

Handel in Dresden

The Deutsche Händel Solisten celebrate their 35th anniversary and that of the 1719 Royal Wedding in Dresden where Handel met Cuzzoni, Durastanti and Senesino who, with Bordoni would later create all the great roles in his operas. So tonight Rheinhard Goebell conducts music from that royal occasion by Lotti, Rebek, Fasch, Schmidt, Telemann and Handel.

Economics?

My flight to Karlsruhe cost £14 but the train to Stansted is £16.50. Returning from Stuttgart to Norwich on frequent flyer miles, the flight is free but the charges are £95.50. Economists may consider their trade a science but the evidence indicates a black art.

Churchill's Thatcher

There is no such thing as society said Mrs Thatcher and Caryl Churchill wrote a play to show that there is. *Top Girls* was written for the Royal Court in 1982 and directed by Max Stafford-Clark whose Chichester revival with Out of Joint has reached Ipswich Wolsey Theatre via the West End. The opening act – a dinner party for iconic women from history – is a prologue for a discussion about a society where the few thrive at the expense of the many. Although the play focuses on the female role in this society, it is not a feminist tract. The message was universal in 1982 and sadly remains so today.

MARCH 2012
Excellence rubbished

Although universally rubbished by the critics, *The Best Exotic Marigold Hotel* is one of the very best films that Jo and I have seen in recent years. I loved the book and I love the film. This is acting finely honed to perfection – as to be expected from Judi Dench, Celia Imrie, Bill Nighy and Maggie Smith.

Judi Dench and Celia Imrie in The Best Exotic Marigold Hotel.

The critics' problem, I suspect, is that it is a feelgood film at a time when explorations of misery are fashionable. But I am an escapist at heart.

Absent friends

Anticipating an evening of catch-up with old design friends, I accept an invitation from the V&A to celebrate the opening of ***Transformation and Revelation – UK Design for Performance 2007-2011***. I meet up with old friends from the Association, of theatre technicians and lighting designers, the Societies of Theatre Research and Theatre Consultants and the Theatres Trust. But designers? Well apart from the Chairmen of the Designers and Lighting Designers – the latter a lighting designer who does a bit of design and direction – there is not a single acquaintance. None of the grandees, none of my students from the 1980s whose work was on show. Sad.

Riccardo Primo (aka Lionheart)

Like any new staging toy, digital projection is full of potential for misuse. But, apart from a couple of minor aberrations, still and video images provide a very powerful contribution to the London Handel Festival production of *Riccardo Primo*. Projecting a series of front cloths rather than painting them is certainly economic but success depends on whether the translucent quality of the image is an appropriate component of the production's scenographic style. Tonight's mediaeval Cyprus is timeless steps with Greek inscriptions on the risers and the cast are costumed in the 18th century of the opera's composition. In this context, the projected video image quality of the video waves, flames and clouds happily complements that of the frontcloths. The stormy sea during the overture is particularly good and a huge rampaging lion neatly solves the perennial problem of big battles on small stages with tiny budgets. Less successful, however, are the disco abstractions added to a pair of arias. Premièred a month after George II ascended the throne, it is inevitable that a libretto about a heroic English King has some jingoistic recits that raise a titter today. But it is full of good music – so good that Handel raided the score's plums for later operas.

Lateral Nutcracking

For a *Nutcracker* choreographer to relocate Christmas Eve from cosy family parlour to Dr Dross' orphanage for Waifs and Strays takes courage

Mathew Bourne's Nutcracker.

and talent. But Matthew Bourne has an abundance of both. His much lauded lateral think reaches Norwich for a full house of us matinee oldies to be enchanted with the energy and confidence that Bourne's dancers bring to this ballet classic. The pathetically stunted Christmas tree and the presents locked way for another year in the cupboard of the barren dormitory ensure true magic as its walls part along a jagged fissure to reveal a frozen lake. The production is strong on transformations using all the old gauze, mist and dry ice tricks that I long for opera directors to adopt. The wit of the choreography is matched by that of the costumes and the confections in Sweetieland are a delight. A truly enjoyable afternoon. Surely there is some little nit to be picked but forgiven? Well, loudspeakers are a poor substitute for a pit band.

APRIL 2012

Forty years on

Throughout the 70s we lived in *The Willows*, a dilapidated timber bungalow among the boatyards on a dyke leading to the River Bure. There was a cut in the garden for our 40 foot historic houseboat and

The Willows.

mooring space for two 20 foot wooden cruisers and a dinghy. For a couple of years, on sabbatical from lighting design, I maintained and hired boats, worked as a casual at Norwich Royal ten miles up the road and made occasional forays to London to teach at RADA. Midlife crisis was averted in an idyllic way. For the rest of the decade I edited, wrote *The Stage Lighting Handbook* and *The Staging Handbook* while lighting a few shows. But when the call to Bury St Edmunds came, there was no alternative to living within ten minutes walk of the theatre.

Forty years on, we have hired a houseboat for a week in that dyke. Old 1920s bungalows like *The Willows* and most of the boatyards have been replaced by expensive houses with luxury gin palace cruisers moored in their gardens. A far cry from the £4000 (1971) price that, being our third move, enabled us to live mortgage free. Fortunately the new houses blend into the environment and we covet each and every one.

Fifty five years on

Our Emerald Wedding. It is Easter Monday Bank Holiday so all the family – children, spouses and grandchildren – are able to join us for grabbits (the family name for buffet lunch). Fiona and Catriona row the

Emerald Wedding Anniversary.

dinghy up and down the dyke as they did as children. And their children have a go. Angus brings scans of photos of all our waterside yesterdays and reminiscences pour forth. Jo and I are alternately bemused by what our marriage vows all these years ago have produced, and proudly content that we have such a happy functional family.

River stalker
Taking a trip up the Bure in the Broads Authority's elegant *Liana* – an exact copy, battery powered, of a historic launch, we do not spot Angus on the river bank so are surprised on checking our email to find photographs of our progress. No coots, once so prolific, in sight.

Down the Bure
A gentle chug through Wroxham and Salhouse Broads on The Queen of the Broads – a name usurped by a serviceable plastic tub from the elegant sleek lined lady of our heyday. Coots at last … few but nesting. And a Muscovy duck appears on the dyke. We liked to think that he is descendent of Grumpy, the Muscovy who lived, fed and bred at the bottom of the garden throughout our 70s sojourn. Great or great great grandchild perhaps?

Broadland dusk
There is something indefinably special about the calm that habitually settles on the Broads most evenings at sunset. The wind drops and the water surface barely ripples providing a canvas for the shadows of the river bank landscape.

Birthday bubbly
Ageing is about little things. My arthritic fingers require the deployment of mechanical advantage (nutcrackers) to loosen the cork before I can ease it out of a prosecco bottle to celebrate my 81st birthday,

Hasse marathon
Advertised as four hours, Hasse's *Cajo Fabricio* lasts five. And that is after cuts. Architecturally and acoustically, Mayfair's Grosvenor Chapel has the right ambience for baroque performance but its pews are a hard sit for old bottoms. Two 15 minute intervals offer a welcome respite – even

if spent queuing for facilities that are considerably less than adequate for an audience with a considerable proportion of the diuretic generation. But these are minor discomforts for such a glorious evening of vocal and instrumental flamboyance from 1732 Rome. Written for six castrati and a tenor, every aria is a show piece, testing, exploiting and demonstrating virtuosity – not just the singers but the instrumentalists, particularly the horns. Tonight we have three counter-tenors, two sopranos, a mezzo and a tenor, with an orchestra of string septet, harpsichord, two oboes doubling recorders and two horns. This ensures a clarity of texture that allows the timbres to tingle. But five hour operas need either a hatchet job on the recitative or the insertion of a long supper interval.

MAY 2012

Statistic Theatre

100% Berlin, 100% Vienna, 100% Vancouver. Now *100% Norfolk.* A cross-section of Norfolk residents – 100 of them – gather on the stage of Norwich Theatre Royal. Devised by every conceivable category including age, sex, occupation, beliefs, geography, education and ethnic origin – particularity whether or not born and bred within Norfolk – the people of our county became statistician's digits. The performing percentagers have brought favourite objects with them and they tell us why. They make statements and the other 99 move to stage left or right according to their agreement, yay or nay. When they (and us) get tired of all this hither and thither, they don and doff sparking red bowler hats to signify their response. With staging requirements of just a pair of video cameras focused on a pair of microphones feeding a projector and circular screen – there is also a feed from a camera on the grid but its views of moving heads could just as well be recorded – this a formula that could well catch on. Could it have potential for that fashionable theatric mantra – outreach? Well, rather than the full houses that are the Saturday matinee norm in Norwich, we percentage watchers were thinly scattered. That was probably the only missing statistic.

Critical first

Workers in the arts know too much about fragility of creative performance to feel comfortable as critics. But never say never, it befits octogenarians to dabble in pastures new. So, when asked to contribute a review of *Riccardo Primo* (p70) to Handel News (the newsletter of the Friends of the London Handel Societally), I had a go and wrote:

The Festival's annual opera staging at the Britten Theatre has become an established highlight of the Handel year, unmissable because most of the chosen operas have not yet entered the expanding Handel repertoire of the major houses. Moreover, pairing emerging singers with the crème de la crème of period musicians under the secure leadership of an international conductor ensures performances that never fail to be exciting and rewarding.

Riccardo Primo was no exception. I loved it in Göttingen and cherish the recording of that 1999 performance. So I approached the Monday performance with anticipation of a pleasurable evening and was not disappointed. The voices – solo and ensemble – rose to the challenge of a score that is full of much better music than received wisdom would lead us to expect.

In general, I find Handel's women to be developed in rather more depth than his men. This opera is no exception. Eleanor Dennis and Emily Renard in the roles premièred by the 'rival queens' found that depth, offering, with their colleagues, ample evidence that the future of Handel singing and acting is in good hands.

Free from the fashionable conceptual fantasises of regietheater, James Robertson Carson directed a straightforward lucid production, faithful to libretto and score. The only moment of confusion was when Costanza fainted during the celebration of her betrothal to Riccardo. Was Eleanor Dennis ill? No, Costanza was distressed at the prospect of marriage to the Lionheart – although scrutiny of score and libretto yields little indication to my ears and eyes.

Like any new staging toy, digital projection is full of potential for misuse. But, apart from a couple of minor aberrations in adding distracting disco effects to a pair of arias, the still and video images provided a very powerful contribution. Projecting a series of front cloths rather than painting them is certainly economic but success depends on the translucent quality of the image being an appropriate component of the production style. With the singers costumed in the 18th century of the opera's composition, Adam Wiltshire's mediaeval Cyprus was timeless steps with Greek inscriptions on the risers. In this context, the video image quality of the waves, flames and clouds happily complemented that of the projected front cloths. The stormy sea during the overture was particularly good and a huge rampaging lion neatly solved the perennial problem of big battles on small stages with tiny budgets.

So, a very enjoyable evening. No quibbles? Well, only very minor. I love the timbre and articulation of keyless wood, valveless brass and gut strings – indeed I regard living thorough the rediscovery of period instruments as one of the joys of my lifetime – but I do occasionally hanker after a touch more flexibility in the pit. Handel's phrases often seem to cry out for the more caressing approach that seems to be more of a general feature of period informed performance in the Eurozone than in London. But I am a Handel hedonist rather than a Handel scholar.

Trousered ladies

Male impersonation is fertile common ground for Opera and Music Hall. In an entertaining exploration, Jessica Walker, with a chair, pianist and hatstand of props, recalls some of the great trousered ladies of the heyday of the halls – with passing reference to the world of Cherubino and Octavian. A slip of a girl with an operatic voice, she lacks the full figure and vocal chords, battered by twice nightly reaching out to the gallery, that bring earthy colour to a double-entendre. But, in the intimacy of Norwich Playhouse, her songs pleasantly recall a faded golden era of popular music theatre.

Patronage

Some five years ago, George Tarbuck shared his concerns with me about the quality of available training in production lighting skills. Observation while working simultaneously in theatres and in theatre education had convinced him that students benefit rather more from placements in real professional situations than in classrooms or even working on student productions. George's ideas resonated strongly with my own feeling that while theatre education has blossomed during

Diploma presentation at Edinburgh School of Lighting and Sound.

my working life, training in technical skills has not kept pace. So I agreed to nail my colours to his mast by attaching my name as patron to his proposed Edinburgh School of Lighting. The commitments of patronage are easy to fulfil: share your enthusiasm for a cause you believe it and make the occasional appearance.

Launching a school from scratch outside the framework of the established educational system is a truly daunting task but, with the support of the local theatres and staging industry, George has established the Edinburgh School of Lighting and Sound and I am in Edinburgh to present the first graduating students with their diplomas. We are in the Royal Lyceum Theatre where I sat as 16-year-old schoolboy in the gods every Saturday night. No one sits in the gods now – my old seat is occupied by a spotlight.

Diva rivalry

Rival Queens.

How real was the rivalry between Handel's 'rival queens', Bordoni and Cuzzonl? Or was it just an invention of the gossip writers? One aspect is for certain – they were the pop celebrities of their day and the satirical press were just as obsessive with them as are today's media. Christopher Benjamin linked the arias with a narrative drawn from the contemporary press, delivering with all the style, vigour and panache of an RSC veteran. Bordoni, Cuzzoni and Handel's other diva, Faustina, were splendidly sung by Maihiri Lawson and Lisa Milne who both responded with witty gestures and facial expressions to the barbed views of 18th century gossip columnists of expensively important foreign sopranos.

Rhythm at the ballet

With their Sinfonia on stage behind them, Northern Ballet dance two hours of Gershwin. Such hits as *Rhapsody in Blue, Summertime, I got plenty o'nuttin, Bess*

Northern Ballet Theatre Gershwin.

you is my woman now, and *I Got Rhythm* – the title of David Dixon's choreographic salute to Broadway. It's great to hear the music deliciously played by a full orchestra with two singers seeped in the black American idiom but it would sound even better if it were not so heavily amplified. A lovely cheerful afternoon.

JUNE 2012

Royal Jubilee

Although having little interest in the daily doings of the royal family, I am a confirmed constitutional monarchist if only because the republic alternative is considerably less appealing. Politicians are a necessity in a democracy that allows divergent opinions. But there has to be a Head of State who is above all the party bickering. Two disconnected thoughts arise from the Diamond Jubilee celebrations. The number of presidential elections that we have been saved during the 60 years of this constitutional monarch – and the replacement by a Thames pageant of a Spithead review of the fleet ('*Standby to reckon up your battleships, ten-twenty-thirty there they go, brag about your cruisers like leviathans, a thousand men a piece down below as we sang at school.*)

Brandenburg boarding

Airlines often display strange musical tastes when selecting music to play during boarding. But what could be more apt than a Brandenburg Concerto for a flight to Leipzig? And on the much maligned – at least by people who don't use it – Ryanair! Booking may be dependent on a finely tuned skill in unticking boxes but the final price, although a multiple of the 'come hither', is usually pretty good as is the on-board experience. However, the fanfare played to boast an on-time arrival is a long way from J. S. Bach.

Händel mit Spärgel

Halle Händelfestspiele coincides with the spärgelsaison and every eatery has a spärgelmenü where every dish features a different way to serve asparagus. Not so long ago, arriving in Halle at 6pm, I would have grabbed a bratwurst from a street stall and hastened to a performance but stamina is one of the fings that aint wot they used to be. So I opt for gentle evening in the hotel restaurant with its lacquered brass remnants of East German grandeur where I wash down my pills with a pils and call not for the speisekarte but the spärgelmenü. Eight very long sticks of white asparagus accompany delicious flaky fish fillets wrapped in wafer thin Westphalian ham. The accompanying sauce boat provides an appropriate concoction of eggs, cream, butter and herbs.

Halle rituals

My first morning of any Halle visit – this the 11th – begins with a tram to the market square (as we approach, the usual nachste halte announcement is varied to welcome visitors to Handel and Halle). It is all now comfortingly familiar in the way that I have grown to appreciate as I have become an oldie. A nod to the flower bedecked statue of GFH on the way to the house where he was born to see this year's special exhibitions and revisit some favourite ephemera. There is always something new on show and the displays are continuously fine-tuned. Zachow – composer, organist, and Handel's first and only teacher – is the subject of this year's special exhibit. Hearing some of his cantatas on the headsets, I make an Amazon order my first priority in returning to the hotel and my computer. But not before the annual ritual of lunch at Hermes where the Greeks offer their Hellenic version of Germanic cuisine – today the pork is cooked with courgettes, aubergines and haloumi cheese

Genserico revived

After composing seven arias, a trio and an overture, Handel abandoned his opera about the fourth century African king who conquered Rome. To complete the story as narrated in tonight's concert, four arias from Telemann's opera on the same subject are interpolated. With the Handel in Italian and the Telemann in German, no guesswork is required as to who wrote what. This allows us to sit back and enjoy rather than indulge in niggling speculation. The aria E già stanca for soprano, violin, harp and lute is alone worth the journey to Halle. The music is played with passion and commitment by a young baroque orchestra. The extended applause is rewarded with two encores before the players finally pick up their music and leave with the applause continuing until the platform is deserted.

Sorcery in the Handel Museum

A young composer has disappeared in the Handel House Museum. His girlfriend is searching for him with the help of a London bobby who is cloned from Spike's funny policeman in the TV series *Wish you were here*. A portrait of *Alcina* comes to life and, yes, she has enslaved him with her magic. *Spuk in Händelhaus* is an hour long adaptation of Alcina for children and they love it as much as I do. (I have seen it three times in the past decade). All the big arias are included except my beloved Tornami and the score sounds great on harpsichord, cello and recorder.

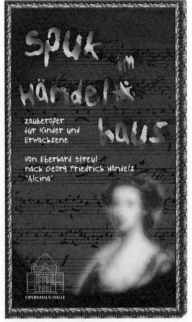

Spuk in Händel Haus flier.

Alcina restructured

Tonight I get my *Tornami* but I have to wait until after the interval for although this *Alcina* has all the arias, they are not – as Eric Morecambe might say – necessarily in the right order. Mucking about like this with such a great Handel opera is dangerously presumptive – especially at a festival in his birthplace. But it has to be said that the dramatic impact is considerably strengthened. Alcina gets to bring the curtain down both at the interval and at the end. Morgana sings *Tornami* in a pursuit of Bradamante culminating in removing his shirt and unwinding what we Osiris Rep husbands know as a 'manly B' to reveal a bra that shatters her love. It all takes place around a swimming pool

Alcina in Halle.

with all of three inches of water into which the ballet dive and swim with great elegance as it slowly elevates some three metres to reveal lovers imprisoned by Alcina's sorcery. There are some nice touches but too many distractingly fidgety ones. I have never heard so much percussion added to a Handel opera but it is discrete and on the whole enhances a top rate musical evening.

Dancing Handel

Labelled a ballet, *Terpsichore* is more a danced cantata as several of the movements are arias, duets and quartets. With *Compagnie Fêtes Galantes* dancing baroque steps reconstructed from period prints and manuals, Les *Talents Lyriques* in the pit and Christophe Rousset conducting – all on the period setting of the 1802 Goethe Theater in Bad Lauchstadt – this was just the afternoon that festivals are made of.

Teseo in Göttingen.

B'Rock

The Ghent period band B'Rock and Middle German Radio Chorus contribute to the loose Lutheran thread running through this year's festival by bridging the music of Catholic and Protestant. Starting with *Dies irae* in plainsong followed by Lully's motet setting, the reformation takes place during the interval for Handel's Foundling Hospital Anthem *Blessed are they that considereth the poor*. This finishes with the Hallelujah Chorus and the composers calling card gets just about the most rousing performance I ever did hear – or perhaps I am just carried away by hearing it in the church where he was baptised and learned to play the organ on the Reichel instrument that is still there. B'rock complete the evening with a spirited account of a concerto grosso.

Oriental baroque

The mutual east-west fascination of the 17th and 18th century is explored by the Pera Ensemble of Istanbul in a morning of *Café Höfische Musik aus Orient und Okzident*. Eleven period instrumentalists covering string quartet, oboe, harpsichord, lute, guitar, ud, and various percussion, plus an alto from Brussels and tenor from Istanbul, play eastern baroque and bring a sympathetically exotic touch to Lully, Popora, Fux, Corelli, Vivaldi and Handel. A wonderful range of textures, timbres and rhythms.

Opernamüsement

I have happy memories of lighting Mozart's one act *Der Schauspieldirektor* at a Bath Festival with Irmgaard Siegfried and Yehudi Menuhin. Leipzig Opera have extended it into a full evening by adding several arias from Salieri and one from Rossini. Describing the result as a *Ein Kabaretisches Opernamüsement*, the action is placed on a platform on the raised pit backed by the displaced orchestra on the elevated mainstage. My knowledge of German can best be described as usually sufficient to ask questions but rarely good enough to understand answers, so I got the visual jokes but few of the verbal ones. Nevertheless I did get the gist of this enjoyable tale of a cynic operatic impresario coping with his divas. It was well sung and the orchestra was the Gewandhaus, no less.

Bach kirken

Before catching the Berlin train for the flight home (should have been the new Brandenburg Airport but opening is delayed – the Germans are mortified at the shadow cast on their efficiency – so it is my final flight from Tegel) there is just time to revisit the two lovely Bach churches where I have fond memories of listening to the cantatas of the great cantor. The Thomaskirche, celebrating its 400 year anniversary, where the cantatas were born and the Nikolaikirche which also came under Bach's wing but is now renowned as the focal point of the wende movement that led to the collapse of east German communist regime and the cold

Leipzig Nikolaikirche.

war wall. The first and only GDR democratic election in 1999 had a 93.54% turnout, which rather puts to shame the current voting apathy for Westminster and local council. In the Thomaskirche, an organist was rehearsing on the new instrument built to a Bach specification and a fine sound it makes

Chigwell birds fly again

The three Chigwell ladies in the sitcom *Birds of a feather* kept us laughing throughout the 90s. Back together after 13 years – this time on stage with a matinee full house of us oldies – they have lost none of their skill to make the most of the farcical situations and double-entendre dialogue.

Birds of a Feather.

Spotlight envy

A quick visit to the annual ABTT Show to say hello to my co-survivors of the not-so-long-ago era of primitive stage technology. I chat and drink Pimms and ignore the high technology on display with one exception – the LED Source Four spotlight. Of all the innovations in the decade since I plotted my last lighting cue, this is the one that I rather wish had been in my tool kit.

JULY 2012

Northern lighting

Overnighting in Manchester en route for the Buxton Festival, I am beset by gloomy memories of trying out musicals 'Immediately prior to London' as the posters trumpeted. *Man of Magic* at the Opera House and *Ambassador* at the Palace, prior to flopping at the Piccadilly and Her Majesty's respectively, became increasingly doom laden with each day of rehearsal. Once open, dwindling audiences were subjected to nightly alterations as words and music were rewritten in a spirit of escalating desperation. Manchester did have some happier lighting moments – such as Stanley Baxter as *Mother Goose*, Harry Worth in *Harvey* and a student *Marriage of Figaro*. But whenever I step off a train at Manchester Piccadilly I am haunted by the spectre of the musical experiences that led to me ringing Jo daily to say that I was giving up lighting design – and, after *Ambassador*, I actually did so for a couple of years.

Pasticcio Armonico

Training weekends for Strand Lighting staff at Buxton Opera House were once a regular feature of my life but until this afternoon I have never seen a show in Matcham's gem. It is a moment worth waiting for. The Armonico Consort's *Too Hot to Handel* is a frothy pasticcio about a boy who hears an opera diva at a concert, falls in love and chances upon her in a park where she has lost her dog. He spots it hovering in the air

Too Hot to Handel.

suspended by a bunch of balloons and on rescuing it, members of Buxton Madrigal Singers pop up around the auditorium to sing the Hallelujah Chorus. The inevitable ups and downs of the relationship are well charted by choosing suitable arias from Handel's vast collection of ecstasy and agony accompanied by string quartet, harpsichord and a discreetly used pair of oboes – an ensemble making a delicious sound, even if unexpected as in *Va tacito e nacosta* without its horns.

Dallying with Intermezzo

Richard Strauss – apart from *Rosenkavalier* and some bits of *Ariadne* – is not really me. However, this Buxton production puts forward a very good case

Intermezzo.

for *Intermezzo's portrayal*, inspired by an incident in the composer's own marriage, of a rather ghastly wife. Janis Kelly gives a bravura performance, the clear production is good to look at and Stephen Barlow's Northern Chamber Orchestra bring out all the gushing lush of the score. Strauss's vocal lines may be great music theatre but I long for an occasional aria and find more musical pleasure in the interludes than in the scenes. I am glad to have seen *Intermezzo* but to see it again would be a da capo too far.

Olympic Vivaldi

Unsurprisingly, Vivaldi's *L'Olimpiade* is popping up at this summer's festivals. The La Serenissima modern dress production sets the opera in what appears to be a sponsor's hospitality tent where the comings and goings centre on the outcome of a single boxing bout on a pair of classically tangled lovers. It all makes lovely listening although there are moments when one yearns just a little for a Bartoli to appear and light the blue touch paper for the firework arias that Vivaldi does so well.

Jeptha

Five chairs and a music stand on a black draped stage, orchestra in the pit, black dressed soloists wandering on during the overture. All the signs of a semi-staged – or, as the Germans call it halbszenisch – production. For the first 20 minutes or so, the soloists come up to the music stand for their arias, pretending to sing from a single score that they pass to each other. The chorus in black, including ruffs of pierrot proportion, are revealed behind a black gauze. So far so good – an easy on the eye concert. Then the director starts tinkering and introduces a ragbag of clichés that were once avant garde – including the inevitable exposure of the back wall and its radiator. There is a glimpse of where a possible concept is coming from but where is the imagination to carry it through? The singers supported by Harry Christophers and The Sixteen rise above the staging and Handel triumphs as always. Mercifully, *Waft her angels through the sky* is allowed to progress in static tableau.

Escape

Avoiding the Olympics – but leaving our TV to record the opening ceremony – we are aboard the cruise ship *Island Escape*. Whisked from

On board Island Escape.

Norwich Airport for embarkation at Palma, we are chugging gently east. The sky is clear, the sun shining, the sea its deepest blue and as calm as the proverbial millpond. No land in sight nor yet a single passing ship. This is a new experience for Jo and I. We have never fancied the traditional rituals associated with cruising, particularly dressing up for formal dinners with strangers. So we have chosen an informal ship with buffet dining and no dress code. The cabin is comfy and so far the nosh has been a pleasure. Altogether, it looks like being a suitable holiday for a couple of oldies with legs past their sell-by date.

Olbia
Seriously hot. Jo declares it the first time she has been warm since before Christmas. Go ashore for a cappuccino and a soupçon of Sardinia.

Napoli
Previous attempts to see inside San Carlo have proved fruitless because of rehearsals. Today they announce visita guida for tomorrow when we shall

be gone. But – after the usual Italian difficulties in finding the ingresso – we visit *MeMus*, the newly opened (October 2011) opera museum. It is an oasis of calm amid the frenzy of Naples and we have it all to ourselves. Interactivity is the current vogue for museum displays and *MeMus* does it with

MeMus.

operatic flair. Supplementing the digital access to the extensive San Carlo archives are a series of 3D video displays using scenic elements from recent productions. Accompanied by impressive surround sound from these productions, these projections are creative works in their own right. Choice is by touch screen pages of the relevant productions poster – which in Italy carries cast and full credits. We enjoyed the Queen of the Night's big act two dazzler, the Ride of the Valkyries and Rossini's Journey to Rheims overture. The original designer models of these productions were on view alongside the costumes and ephemera that are the heart of a theatre museum. The opening of *MeMus* has generated a beautifully illustrated book that I shall cherish.

Cittavechia

I have been to Rome but Jo has not. So we sign up for an afternoon of *Relaxing Rome – Easy on the Legs* and are whisked around the key monuments in the air-conditioned comfort appropriate for octogenarians on a scorching July day.

Propriano

Take a coach tour of southern Corsica's spectacular mountains, visiting a couple of villages. Jo on a high from French tour guide complimenting her on being so beautifully dressed (charity shop skirt, Matalan blouse … but rather splendid straw hat bought on-board last night). Although I am familiar with the workings of that great bit of wooden stage technology, the *corsican trap*, the phrase acquires an entire new meaning when I find myself in a loo with a defective lock.

Ocean Theatre

Every evening offers free twice nightly show but Elvis, Young Talent and Lloyd Webber have seemed a poor alternative to Mediterranean sunsets (first house) and bed (second house).

Propriano.

But our week is passing and being compulsive theatregoers, we decide – with some trepidation for neither Jo nor I ever rocked or rolled – to take a punt on *Rocking round the world*. We need not have feared. Only the opening rocked. The show was a sequence of production numbers from the heyday of the Summer Show. Yes, there was a can-can and a carnival in Rio and a cringingly jingoistic finale that was pure music hall patriotism –*There always be an England* (when I was a wartime schoolboy we always added *as long as Scotland's there*), *Land of Hope and Glory*, and *Rule Britannia*. Yes, the costumes did open to reveal union jacks.

Menorca

Having had half-a-dozen holidays in Menorca, this is the great deja vu of the cruise, although we have never before experienced entering the great natural harbour from the sea – the reason that Nelson colonised it and gave it Georgian sash windows. Saunter familiar streets, sangria in the Plaza Reial, listen to the magnificent 1809 organ in Santa Maria, paella for lunch.

Palma

Wake up in Palma for a seven o'clock breakfast and are back in Norwich for a one o'clock lunch. It has been a super week – both relaxing and stimulating – the answer to decreasing mobility.

Olympic opening

Home to a recording of the Olympics opening ceremony and, wow, is it a lavish spectacular! Awash with imagination and every pound of the £27 million budget visible. The industrial revolution with chimneys growing through Blake's green and pleasant land is a masterstroke of scenic transformation. And how about the cauldron!

AUGUST 2012

Dancing the Play

Having enjoyed Matthew Bourne's Play without words at the National in 2002, Jo and I hastened to its revival – on tour in Norwich – to mark 25 years of his New Adventures company. Set in 1965 and inspired by British cinema of that era, particularly Losey's film of Pinter's *The Servant*, *Play without words* is a successful exploration of new possibilities of developing both narrative and character without recourse to dialogue. Although Bourne's wordless play is not dance, it uses the techniques of the ballet to act a story through movement and music. With three actors to each principal role, multifaceted aspects of personality are revealed simultaneously and the action carried forward in satisfying visual patterns. The jazz score for quintet of clarinets/saxophone, trumpet/flugelhorn, double bass, percussion and keyboards both underscores the action and enters into a dialogue with the movement. The result is contemporary theatre at its best.

Olympic closing

Never having been a sports spectator, nor indeed a participator, I have not been an avid follower of the Olympic pursuit of physical excellence. Nevertheless, the level of media coverage has ensured a consistent awareness of particularly outstanding performances and the medal count. The closing ceremony, like the opening, was a magnificent piece of staging for which my gold medal goes to lighting designer Patrick Woodroffe. However, born optimist, as I most certainly I am, I find it difficult to believe the idea promoted by politicians and media that London 2012 heralds a new great age for Britain.

Cyberflöte

Tonight's Salzburg Festival *Die Zauberflöte* is being shown throughout Europe and beyond. I am in Norwich's Cinema City. The 1982 Flute that I saw in Salzburg's 17th century Felsentreitschule was a highpoint in my life. How can a new production in the Felsentreitschule surpass the magic of that evening? Visually it cannot and it does not try. Vocally it meets the challenge and the period reading of Concentus Musicus is on a par with the Vienna Philharmonic while providing an excitingly alternative sound. Costumed in a somewhat caricatured version of today, the production is reasonably faithful to Shikaneder's scenario while introducing some imaginative detailing. The serpent is a long slithering snake that the three ladies introduce into Tamino's bedroom and then don nurse's caps to cure him. Papageno enters driving a three wheeler delicatessen and sings *Der vogelfänger bin ich ja* surrounded by a bevy of choreographed female customers with baskets eager to buy his game birds. Monostatos is more credible than usual as indeed are the youthful Pamina and Tamino. But the fire and water are routinely portrayed – there is not much magic around. Saratsro presides over a chorus of white coats who tick boxes on their clipboards. Rather than join this brotherhood, Tamino, Pamina, Papageno and Papagena, pushing the four prams that appeared during the *Pa, pa, pa* duet, go off into the sun leaving Saratstro strangling the Queen of the Night as the stage blacks out on the last note. Whatever became of the enlightenment?

Nae wind

Arrive in Edinburgh by rail rather than customary Flybe to discover that the famed wind up the *Waverley steps* is a now but a memory. Where once I battled seemingly endless flights of steps against the wind, an enclosed escalator carries me sedately upwards to Princes Street and the hotel that carries so many memories of lighting pantos at the King's. My room looks out on a panorama extending from the Castle to Arthur's seat. Memories, memories!

Greyfriars – Bobby and Kirk

I grew up in an Edinburgh culture which tended to regard pubs as dens of depravity. So my first tentative venture within a public house was fraught with teenage trepidation. Returning tonight to that pub – *Greyfriars Bobby* – and inevitably finding it gentrified, I rise to the occasion by ordering not a pint of Heavy but a half of Peroni. I am en route to Greyfriars Kirk for Iestyn Davies singing Handel and Porpora. Apart from a short Handel violin sonata, this is an evening of lover's angst beautifully sung ... once again I rejoice in being alive in the age of the rediscovery of the male alto voice.

Fringe punting
Always intending to read Mrs Oliphant – Edinburgh's Jane Austen – but never getting around to it, I take punt on a dramatisation of *Miss Marchbanks* playing in one of the vaulted cellars that underpin Georgian Edinburgh. Scanning the director notes and actor biogs in the programme feeds a suspicion of over-researching and under-casting. And so this turns out to be. Even with acting at the bottom end of the amdram scale it might have just about survived with some attempt at Scottish accents – polite Edinburgh lady is not all that difficult. When, 20 minutes before the end, while the 99th cup of tea is poured in the drawing room, my diuretics kick in (fringe drama rarely has an interval). I creep out and do not return. But I renew my vow to read Mrs Oliphant and buy a copy.

Masks dell' arte
Wonderful display of masks by Renzo Antonello at the Italian Cultural Institute, supported by a brilliant 20 minute Commedia dell' Arte performance by Charioteer Theatre. Such pure theatre that I cannot overstate my enthusiasm.

Gay Handel
Va Tacito will never quite be the same again after the *Philhomoniker* (Munich Gay men Choir) *Guilio Cesare in Egito*. A few splendidly send-up-camp moments a la Frankie Howerd such as Tolomeo's "I've always wanted to walk like an Egyptian" but mostly just a tongue-in-cheek view of Caesar's sojourn in Cleopatra's Egypt. Well sung, great fun, no scenery but costumes with a detachable panels that combine to provide a projection surface for witty comments. Not entirely surprisingly, the director is a cheerful young girl.

Middle East conflict
An evening of gorgeous textures from William Christie's Arts Florissants in Charpentier's *David et Jonathas*. The sound from 24 strings and ten

winds is lush but crisply articulated. With less prominent differentiation between aria and recitative than in the German or Italian styles, French baroque flows with a continuity that is rare before Wagner. In tonight's production, a pine box expands and contacts, horizontally and vertically, to provide a flexible setting. While some changes seem indicative of claustrophobia, most – and there are many – elude me. But I can take this sort of thing in my stride as soon as I recognise a production that would be billed as 'abandon logic all ye who enter in' if opera houses were subject to normal trading standards. Just as I anticipate the likelihood of directors exploiting any hint of homoeroticism in what appears to be written as a purely platonic friendship. Throughout *David et Jonathas* there is much talk of peace but, seeped in television, we are all aware of the inevitability of any middle east story ending in conflict. Any war is ghastly but this one was beautifully sung.

  [PS: Reviewing David et Jonathas *in* The Times, *Richard Morrison writes of how the staging "takes a moderately complicated old testament story and makes it completely baffling" with "walls zooming in and out as if auditioning for the hokey-kokey"]*

Un petit voyage baroque française

Morning concerts provide some of my particularly special memories of 65 years of Edinburgh Festivals and Arts Florissant's survey of the development of French baroque opera certainly earns its memory cell. Presented as a journey from Cambert (*Pomone*, 1671) through Lully (*Achille et Polyxène*, 1687), Grabu (*Albion and Albanius*, 1684), Charpentier (*Mèdèe*, 1693) to Rameau (*Les Indes Galantes* 1735), Paul Agnew – distinguished countertenor successfully turning his hand to conducting – provides a potted evolutionary timeline. As the rediscovery of 18th century opera increasingly embraces the genre of the French court, this concert offers a useful clarification. With French baroque pursuing a different sound from the rest of Europe, the timbre of flûtes à bec, whether combined with oboes or not, makes a particularly tingling contribution to the orchestral texture.

SEPTEMBER 2012

Olympic Summer

Never having been one for competitive sport, playing or watching, my participation in the Olympics has been restricted to the televised opening and closing ceremonies which certainly scored gold for showbiz. The biggest ooh-ah moment was the sprouting of the chimneys of the industrial revolution.

Subdued PLASA

The annual jamboree for the makers and users (i.e. sellers and buyers) of lighting and sound equipment is showing signs of recession. Fewer exhibitors on less lavish stands and a bias toward "me too" variations rather than risky innovation. But although there are wider aisles, it is still difficult to navigate with a map giving each stand a grid reference when the aisles display no indication of co-ordinates. However, although this is irritating, it of little consequence to one whose visits, once a hectic round of seeking out new toys, reviewing them for magazines and speaking at seminars has become a gentle saunter, gossiping with fellow oldies and presenting the Francis Reid award of the Association of Lighting Designers to this year's likely lad, whom I am delighted to find is a graduate of the Royal Conservatoire of Scotland.

Convivial Fellows

Dining in the intimacy of the Elgar Room of the Savile Club with the Fellows of the ABTT, I feel – for the first time in my life – rather like an elder statesman. Seated with a dozen of the key innovators of 20th century stage technology, I am conscious of just how small was my input to these revolutionary years. My role was largely that of facilitator – spreading the word by writing and teaching. There is a rhythm to these events. Over drinks, we exchange updates on our current activities and the meal is a time for reminiscences. By the coffee we are ready for the topic that we are by our aged status least qualified to discuss – the future. A convivial evening marred only by absence of the ladies, none of whom to the shame of the ABTT have been elected fellows.

OCTOBER 2012

Birthday Bash

Back at the Savile for John Offord's 70th birthday. We are summoned to ascend the grand staircase to dine in the splendours of the ballroom by Malcolm Arnold's fanfare for trumpet duet, composed for the 1968 centenary of the Brook Street club. This is the street where Handel lived so between courses we have *Let the Bright Seraphim* with trumpet obbligato and my favourite *Tornami a vagheggiar* from *Alcina*. John has made a very substantial contribution to theatre by publishing, organising exhibitions, and generally being a cheerful animateur. From hot metal to laser via litho, his publishing has encompassed the launch of such magazines as Municipal Entertainment and Lighting + Sound International. Now his Entertainment Technology news appears in print and on-line. He had a major role in the development of PLASA but his crowning acquirement must surely be his early realisation the potential of publish-on-demand to establish Entertainment Technology Press to meet the need for specialist books about theatre production techniques. The list, built up over 14 years now stands at over 75 – all available in print or as kindle e-books.

Choreographed Caesar

Dance company Fabulous Beast have a prominent role in new ENO Julius Caesar directed by Michael Keegan-Dolan. For the first ten minutes or so I have an uneasy feeling we are about to experience an entry to the Eurovision Song Contest but the choreography soon departs from an initial quasi-ABBA response to the rhythm and makes an interesting, often fascinating, comment on the progress of Caesar's adventures in Egypt. The dancing mostly runs in parallel with the singing – interaction is relatively rare. This Julius Caesar enjoys big game hunting so a crocodile awaits on stage as we enter the auditorium and a giraffe appears later. Both are subjected to rituals that belong to an abattoir rather than a stage. The desert is suggested by vast expanses of chipboard and plywood. The singers mostly just stand still and sing their arias to the audience while the dancers

Julius Caesar at ENO.

respond physically to the music. None of the goings on offer me any new insight on an opera that I am very familiar with although playing Sesto as a daughter rather than son is an interesting experiment that works. Lawrence Zazzo, Tim Mead, Patricia Bardon and Anna Christy lead a strong cast and Christopher Curnyn once again demonstrates that he is in the top echelon of baroque conductors. I shall return to the revival.

Sixties Figaro

Updating opera inevitably introduces anomalies but in case of *The Marriage of Figaro* these are relatively few, especially as there is a current school of thought that regards droit *de signeur* as a myth. Glyndebourne's latest production of the opera that opened both their old and new opera houses is set in the Moorish architecture of an Andalusian palazzo. The location may be 60s Seville but the characters have a distinct flavour of 60s Sussex. No harm in that, Beaumarchais and da Pointe only placed the story in Spain to limit censorship resulting from its revolutionary aspects. Surprisingly, as there were creepy musicians and clerics aplenty in the 60s, the only character who fails to make the transition is Basilo. The touring cast is strong with a particularly good Almaviva. However the narrow proscenium in Norwich provides an unacceptable sightline problem in Act 2 that could have avoided by some relatively minor re-blocking. But, all-in-all, a most satisfactory evening.

NOVEMBER 2012

Bookmaking

Since life is peppered with inevitabilities, it is not surprising that I have written a book about Handel or, to be more accurate, put together a book about Handel. I could not ask John Offord to publish a book so remote from theatre technology and I am too old to hawk it around. So I have turned DIY publisher.

Constriction stabilised

An echo scan of my heart confirms no further hardening of my pericardium since 2010. So my cardiology clinic visits can be annual rather than six monthly. So there's life in the old dawg yet.

More Mathew Magic

Matthew Bourne's approach is consistently lateral, his choreography consistently witty and his productions consistently theatrical. When he rethinks a classic, his approach is innovative but always respectful of the original concept, its scenario and its music. His Gothic reworking of *Sleeping Beauty* moves not towards betrothal, wedding and happy ever after but to bed, baby and happy ever after. Born in 1890, the year of the ballet's première, his Aurora grows into an Edwardian princess and awakens today from her century sleep. A lovely magical matinee. I shall forever cherish the baby Aurora – puppet but 99% realistic – crawling over the stage and climbing the curtains.

DECEMBER 2012

Sixties Goldoni

Although Goldoni was developing a more verbal theatre, *Servant of Two Masters* still has its roots in commedia dell'arte. Finding a way to present early drama to today's audience often results in an acting style that aims for elegance but descends into camp. But Nicholas Hytner's direction of Richard Bean's reworking of Goldoni's comedy masterpiece as *One Man, Two Guvnors* gets it wonderfully right – and earns the National Theatre a big, big critical and commercial hit. Set in a 1960s Brighton peopled by some very dodgy characters culled from seaside postcards, carry on films, Whitehall farce and panto, the pace of the verbal and visual comedy is frantic. The action is punctuated by hilarious set-pieces which the audience applaud as if arias in an opera. Incidental music is provided by a quartet dressed like an early boy band in matching suits, ties and haircuts. With guitars, washboard and period microphones, they cover scene changes by perform Grant Olding period pastiche songs in frontcloth. I loved it all.

Concerned about controlling her cough in the aftermath of a cold, Jo stayed at home but the laughter of the scholars and oldies at a Norwich midweek matinee was so continuous that she need not have worried about breaking silent moments of dramatic tension. (Writing this reminds of Ralph Richardson's remark that "Acting is merely the art of keeping a large number of people from coughing").

Bronchial absence

Yesterday I should have been at the Barbican for *Belshazzar* and today at the New London theatre for ABTT Christmas conviviality. But I am laid low with dysfunctional lungs while antibiotics trounce a seasonal virus. So the oratorio is recorded Trevor Pinnock rather than live William Christie and the ABTT is toasted in absentia.

Ego boost

My ego is surprised but delighted to learn from a review by Jim Laws that my new book 'reveals a superbly tuned pair of ears and an able brain between them to translate aural experiences into accessible text'. But I doubt whether the Arts Council will heed his advice to 'make this book compulsory reading for any of their clients who want to produce Handel for the first time'.

Christmas

Santa Claus brought me Handel's *Hercules*.

Hogmanay

This is the 56th midnight that Jo and I have seen in a new year together. Graham 1985 is in our glasses as we toast each other and family (in absentia) with

> *Here's tae us, Wha's like us, Gie few, an they're a' deid*

JANUARY 2013

Peter Ebert

Peter died on Hogmanay. There were gie few like him. Having inherited his father's charm, he was a delight to work with. During much of my Glyndebourne decade he was responsible for the revivals of the productions on which he had originally assisted The Professor (as we all addressed Ebert senior). With the original casts being gradually replaced during the 60s, these revivals increasingly developed from what the German theatre calls wiederaufname (literally a resumption – an identical copy) to neueinstudierung (newly studied) approach. Any design imposes a production style and this was particularly so with Oliver Messel's sets and costumes. But within this environmental framework, Peter had a flair for developing the characters to suit the particular talents of individual singers. And he encouraged me to re-think the lighting, taking advantage of the advances in technique and technology that were such an exciting feature of the 60s. Our biggest success was the 1964 *Idomeneo* – and not just because Pavarotti sang Idamante – while our biggest flop was the 1966 musical *Man of Magic*. This was a fairly traumatic experience for both of us (see *Hearing the Light*, pages 112-115). Amid the rewrites, rescores, reorders, cuts and adds of the Manchester tryout, Peter turned to me at the production desk saying "how can we claim to do original versions of old operas … it was probably like this!" He was truly one of the gie few.

Waltzing with Wagner

It is bicentenary year for Verdi and Wagner. So the Viennese New Year concert relayed from the Musikverein peppers its traditional waltzes with a spot of *Lohengrin* and *Don Carlo*. The plum is a quadrille (Strauss? Lanner?) full of goodies from *Rigoletto*, *Macbeth* and *Ernani*.

Hibernation

From the first to the thirsty first, the best way to to deal with winter depth is to follow the lead of the dormouse. No need to go anywhere or doing anything so lapse into preservative lethargy.

Mozart Trilogy

I first heard Mozart 39 when I was 16. It was 1947 – the first Edinburgh Festival – the orchestra was the Vienna Philharmonic and the conductor Bruno Walter. It has remained my favourite ever since, beating 40 and 41 by the breadth of the finest gossamer hair. That these three glorious symphonies were composed by Mozart in his spare time during a period of just six weeks is a feat beyond any available adjective. I never managed to catch one of the very rare occasions when all three are played in sequence until a Scottish Chamber Orchestra concert in 2007 (see *Carry on Fading*, p69). That was on modern instruments, albeit with natural horns and trumpets – but now my yearning to hear a performance on the instruments that Mozart wrote for has been satisfied by Simon Rattle and the Orchestra of the Age of Enlightenment. And how! Clearly articulated by gut strings and keyless wind, from the first chord of 39 with the sharp bite of timpani played with hard stick to the complex tapestry of the Jupiter finale that is the culmination of the 18th century symphony, this was an evening that lived up to a lifetime expectation. Oh, let there be a CD.

FEBRUARY 2013

Downsizing

Jo and I have cardio-vascular systems that need daily medication cocktails to keep them marginally fit for purpose. My hands have succumbed to arthritis and Jo's eyes provide only peripheral vision. The Stuart Road house – end terrace with add-ons – suddenly seems impossibly big and its staircase an increasing challenge. So we put it on the market on Thursday, sell it on Friday afternoon and buy a ground floor flat on Saturday morning. So much for the stagnant housing market.

Nomadic

House moves were a regular feature of our life until we settled in Norwich in 1989. We began married life briefly in a Notting Hill Gate bedsit before renting a basement in Hampstead's Vale of Health for £2.50 per week. Then we bought our first house – £1,650 with an £82.75 deposit – newly modernised in a Lewes Terrace. Three years later we found a delightful country cottage in Laughton and stayed there for the rest of my Glyndebourne decade. At the end of the 60s our instincts took us to the East Anglia that we had fallen in love with, particularly while working at the Aldeburgh Festival and holidaying on the Norfolk Broads – firstly to Maldon where we had honeymooned and then for most of the 70s to the Broads. The Willows was a 1920 timber bungalow in Hoveton (across the bridge from Wroxham) with a frontage to a dyke off the River Bure. Most of the wooden piles which provided its foundations had rotted away and it floated on old railway sleepers. The survey described the house, if not the site, as a negative asset. Buying for £4000 and living mortgage free, we ran Willow Boats – two cruisers and a houseboat –

from the bottom of the garden. I worked the winters at Norwich Theatre Royal and wrote my first two books. Then the icy blast of Thatcherism forced a retreat from the hazard of freelance fees to the safety of salaried jobs, first at the Theatre Royal in Bury St Edmunds then Central School of Art & Design. So we moved to Bury and then to Wivenhoe with its commuter line to London. Being away from Norfolk for a decade made us certain that we wanted to end our days there. Stuart Road, with its easy access to rail, airport and theatre was intended to be our last resting place. So we extended and renovated. But our diminishing mobility now needs a simpler cocoon that will also serve for the inevitability of one of us outliving the other. As to which one that shall be, the odds are currently even.

Ephemera

I have always been an accumulator of paper. The documentary remains of a lifetime in theatre have already gone to the archives of the Royal Conservatoire of Scotland. Now the reference books and ring bound ephemera of a traveller and writer must be decimated. Every programme of every play, musical, opera and concert must go – except those of my own productions and those of Handel – each examined and its triggered memory savoured before consignment to the bin. Cuttings, fliers, leaflets follow. Then books – out, out except theatre architecture, Handel and baroque. Meanwhile Jo attacks the lifetime accumulation of bric-a-brac. Family are encouraged to take their pick and loads are shuttled to charity shop. Is it sad to jettison all this memorabilia? No, it's strangely exhilarating – a beginning rather than an end.

Baroque Francaise

It took me a long time – about 50 years – to tune my ear to French baroque with its seemingly endless recitative punctuated by arias that fail to stir the blood and dance music played with genteel correctness and subjected to anaemic choreography. But the period instrument movement and its associated research has changed all that. The musical treasures of Versailles are now revealed as good theatre. Rameau, Charpentier & Co are following Handel, Vivaldi & Co into the repertoire. Having toed the water with Rameau ENO have now turned to Charpentier with a dream team – conductor Christian Curnyn, director David McVicar, choreographer Lynne Page, designer Bunny Christie and Lighting Designer Paule Constable – who have come up roses. *Medea* is a tragedy and the splendid Sarah Conolly grasps all the complex nuances of the doomed heroine. But the context is rather more Hollywood musical than ancient Greece. The war is that of 1939 with a chorus plotting troop movements on a map table in château ops room. Delightful choreography embraces rhythms that are anything but courtly and the pit is awash with delicious timbres.

MARCH 2013

Lifestyle pacing

Going to *Medea* has made me realise that my mobility has decreased to the point that London visits are no longer much fun. Despite taking things easy, including an overnight hotel, I return to Norwich so knackered that I have embarked on a lifestyle review. Serious? Well, I have sent back my London Handel Festival tickets.

Showlight snuffed

And, after much agonising, I have withdrawn from the Showlight conference at Cesky Krumlov in May. My paper on "Living through a Lighting Revolution" was to have been my final words on lighting design – my swansong. But I have to confront realism and settle for being a mute swan.

Cosi

Our annual Arts Council opera ration in Norwich is a week of Glyndebourne and half a week of English Touring Opera. Comparisons may be odious but they are inevitable. Both are strong on ensemble although Glyndebourne tends to score on voices. But ETO has a better band and fewer doolally directors. Tonight's Cosi is concept free, played as Mozart and da Ponte wrote it, with a director who supports rather than interprets and a conductor who relishes the score and draws beautiful phrasing from his musician. If da Ponte had written a sequel, I am sure he would have provided the girls with lovers worthy of them.

Siege of Calais

The rarity of Donizetti's *Siege of Calais* is attributed to a third act below par on all counts, musically and dramatically. So ETO chopped the last act, cherry picking a couple of arias to insert in previous scenes. As musically cheerful as his comedies, Donizetti

ETO Siege of Calais.

tragedies are full of toe-tapping rhythms just right for marching along in the face of adversity. Another overlooked work worthy of a place in the repertoire. I'd certainly go to see it again.

APRIL 2013

Icy Easter

March broke records for snow and icy blasts and, while April has brought sunshine, the temperature is barely above freezing, the wind chill ensures that any venture out-of-doors requires furry gloves and woolly hat. Not imagining that winter would be so extended, we have booked a repeat of last year's Easter week on the houseboat Marinella moored opposite The Willows where we lived through the 70s. Setting out for the river with more than a little trepidation, we are delighted to find ourselves cosily cocooned. Easter Monday falls on April 1st and children and grandchildren arrive for the traditional family buffet known as grabbits. And the resident Heron awaits his sardines.

Did nothing in particular but did it superbly well

The week has passed in enjoying the minute-by-minute variations in the Broadland sky and water. The sun has shone but the wind has bitten. The biggest exertion has been collecting the *Eastern Daily Press* and feeding the aquatic wildlife. This kind of relaxation is an essential life skill that Jo and I have honed to perfection.

From heights to depths

Fiona and Kayleigh join us for a measuring session in the new flat and we celebrate our 56th wedding anniversary with a bottle of prosecco. They agree that the flat is just right for us. We plan an exciting future. Then comes a devastating phone call. The buyer for 20 Stuart Road has withdrawn and we are back on the market. This triggers our loss of the flat.

Black Watch

I have been looking forward to catching up with the smash hit that established the National Theatre of Scotland and following years of international touring is coming to Norwich. But, as my letter to the box office explains.

Thank you for today's e-mail notification of the parameters for the Black Watch performances. Sadly, as an 82 year old dependent on a daily cocktail of diuretics, I cannot contemplate a two hour seated stretch. There is considerable certainty that I would have to leave the auditorium during the second hour and I have no wish to disturb the audience in this way. (You, correctly, would not let me return to my seat, doubling the disturbance.)

Consequently, I feel that I have no alternative but to abandon my plan to attend and therefore return my tickets in case you are able to resell them to someone who otherwise might not be able to attend this outstanding production.

Disabled access is not just a structural matter of substituting ramps for steps.

Angelic dragons

Jo has written a little poem that I relate to. She is a touch concerned that it may be blasphemous – well she is a grandchild of the vicarage.

> *Some people they have angels*
> *To help them on their way*
> *But I have little dragons*
> *To pass the time of day.*
> *They sing a lot and laugh a lot*
> *And splash in seas of flame.*
> *I think that people's angels*
> *Are really just the same.*

Caesar from the Met

Universally acknowledged since its 2005 Glyndebourne première as a particularly fine production, David McVicar's update of *Guilo Cesare in Egito* from the Roman Empire of first century BC to the British Empire of the 19th AD has now conquered the Met. Choreographing the rhythmic arias in a style owing more to the traditions of vaudeville than opera, McVicar takes a huge risk but pulls it off with such confidence that, for the duration of the performance, it seems the only way. Of course, while being by no means the only way to stage such a multifaceted masterpiece, it certainly is a very convincing response to the music.

Daniele de Niese as Handel's Cleopatra.

The original production raised Daniele de Niese from star to diva. Could another of the great Handel sopranos pull it off? Nathalie Dessay sure does. She is an older, more mature, Cleopatra who, while almost matching the de Niese 'out front' sparkle, brings more depth to the arias of despair. I prefer my Caesar to be a male alto rather than female one and David Daniels is very convincing, as are Patricia Bardon's Cornelia, Alice Coote's Sesto, and Christophe Dumaux's Tolomeo. They all sing admirably and Harry Bicket produces a rich but period sound (gorgeous horns) from the Met orchestra. I suspect that I experienced a better afternoon in the intimacy of my local 170 seater cinema than I would have done in the vastness of the Met.

MAY 2013

Limbo

May Day and the view from my desk is dominated by a forlorn For Sale board that has attracted only two viewers in the three weeks since we returned to the market. The future is on hold. We live for today, unable to plan for tomorrow. Alternative estate agents are hovering – mailing, phoning and doorstepping – to offer their allegedly superior marketing skills. One likely lad, flourishing confidence in his employer, rather spoilt his pitch by leaving a proposal pack that inadvertently included an internal memo detailing the complaints of a dissatisfied client. [Or was it inadvertent? – as I noted in mailing the memo back to him "unless you wished to re-assure me that, while every organisation has an occasional cock-up, heaven, earth and the regional director will always be moved to handle legitimate complaints"]. Meanwhile I have informed my current sole agency that while I remain confident that they will find a buyer, I think that it may be prudent to consider a review of the situation in mid-May if the present dearth of interest by prospective buyers continues. Then at least I would have a different sale board to contemplate from my window.

SUMMER 2013

Halle Handel Festival cancelled on the eve of catching flight. Holiday postponed while we await prospective buyers. Eventually get a sale and buy an over-55 retirement ground floor flat in Wroxham – a few steps to the river and over the bridge to Roy's "World's biggest village department store".

AUTUMN 2013

Move in on 20th August. Within a few days, I collapse and spend the autumn in and out of Norfolk and Norwich University Hospital culminating in open heart surgery at Papworth Hospital to remove calcium deposits from the pericardium protective sac around my heart. After rehab in North Walsham cottage hospital I am home for Christmas.

WINTER 2013/14

Home for Christmas but collapse on December 28th and spend six weeks in cardiology on intermittent blood transfusion while they try to discover source of blood loss. With X-ray, CT scan, Angiogram and swallowed cameras, it is traced to a leaking artery and cauterised. After intensive physiotherapy to get me walking again I am discharged.

SPRING 2014
Slowly restored to a stable "normality" with reduced mobility. The aftermath of prolonged hospital stay is non-functional bladder muscles requiring a catheter for life.

SUMMER 2014
With Angus taking us to Harwich and Fiona bringing us back to Wroxham, we cruise on *Brilliance of the Seas* to Copenhagen, Tallinn, St Petersburg, Stockholm, Visby and Oslo. Finger distortion, thought to be arthritis now diagnosed as Gout.

Zimmer me.

On board Brilliance of the Seas.

ENTERTAINMENT TECHNOLOGY PRESS

FREE SUBSCRIPTION SERVICE

Keeping Up To Date with

Fading into Retirement

Entertainment Technology titles are continually up-dated, and all major changes and additions are listed in date order in the relevant dedicated area of the publisher's website. Simply go to the front page of www.etnow.com and click on the BOOKS button. From there you can locate the title and be connected through to the latest information and services related to the publication.

The author of the title welcomes comments and suggestions about the book and can be contacted by email at:
francisreid@btinternet.com

110 Fading into Retirement

Titles Published by Entertainment Technology Press

50 Rigging Calls *Chris Higgs, Cristiano Giavedoni 246pp* **£16.95**
ISBN: 9781904031758
Chris Higgs, author of ETP's two leading titles on rigging, An Introduction to Rigging in the Entertainment Industry and Rigging for Entertainment: Regulations and Practice, has collected together 50 articles he has provided regularly for Lighting + Sound International magazine from 2005 to date. They provide a wealth of information for those practising the craft within the entertainment technology industry. The book is profusely illustrated with caricature drawings by Christiano Giavedoni, featuring the popular rigging expert Mario.

ABC of Theatre Jargon *Francis Reid 106pp* **£9.95** ISBN: 9781904031093
This glossary of theatrical terminology explains the common words and phrases that are used in normal conversation between actors, directors, designers, technicians and managers.

Aluminium Structures in the Entertainment Industry *Peter Hind 234pp* **£24.95**
ISBN: 9781904031062
Aluminium Structures in the Entertainment Industry aims to educate the reader in all aspects of the design and safe usage of temporary and permanent aluminium structures specific to the entertainment industry – such as roof structures, PA towers, temporary staging, etc.

AutoCAD – A Handbook for Theatre Users *David Ripley 340pp* **£29.95**
ISBN: 9781904031741
From 'Setting Up' to 'Drawing in Three Dimensions' via 'Drawings Within Drawings', this compact and fully illustrated guide to AutoCAD covers everything from the basics to full colour rendering and remote 3D plotting. Third, completely revised edition, June 2014.

Automation in the Entertainment Industry – A User's Guide *Mark Ager and John Hastie 382pp* **£29.95** ISBN: 9781904031581
In the last 15 years, there has been a massive growth in the use of automation in entertainment, especially in theatres, and it is now recognised as its own discipline. However, it is still only used in around 5% of theatres worldwide. In the next 25 years, given current growth patterns, that figure will rise to 30%. This will mean that the majority of theatre personnel, including directors, designers, technical staff, actors and theatre management, will come into contact with automation for the first time at some point in their careers. This book is intended to provide insights and practical advice from those who use automation, to help the first-time user understand the issues and avoid the pitfalls in its implementation.

Basics – A Beginner's Guide to Lighting Design *Peter Coleman 92pp* **£9.95**
ISBN: 9781904031413
The fourth in the author's 'Basics' series, this title covers the subject area in four main sections: The Concept, Practical Matters, Related Issues and The Design Into Practice. In an

area that is difficult to be definitive, there are several things that cross all the boundaries of all lighting design and it's these areas that the author seeks to help with.

Basics – A Beginner's Guide to Special Effects *Peter Coleman 82pp* **£9.95**
ISBN: 9781904031338
This title introduces newcomers to the world of special effects. It describes all types of special effects including pyrotechnic, smoke and lighting effects, projections, noise machines, etc. It places emphasis on the safe storage, handling and use of pyrotechnics.

Basics – A Beginner's Guide to Stage Lighting *Peter Coleman 86pp* **£9.95**
ISBN: 9781904031208
This title does what it says: it introduces newcomers to the world of stage lighting. It will not teach the reader the art of lighting design, but will teach beginners much about the 'nuts and bolts' of stage lighting.

Basics – A Beginner's Guide to Stage Sound *Peter Coleman 86pp* **£9.95**
ISBN: 9781904031277
This title does what it says: it introduces newcomers to the world of stage sound. It will not teach the reader the art of sound design, but will teach beginners much about the background to sound reproduction in a theatrical environment.

Basics: A Beginner's Guide to Stage Management *Peter Coleman 64pp* **£7.95**
ISBN: 9781904031475
The fifth in Peter Coleman's popular 'Basics' series, this title provides a practical insight into, and the definition of, the role of stage management. Further chapters describe Cueing or 'Calling' the Show (the Prompt Book), and the Hardware and Training for Stage Management. This is a book about people and systems, without which most of the technical equipment used by others in the performance workplace couldn't function.

Building Better Theaters *Michael Mell 180pp* **£16.95** ISBN: 9781904031406
A title within our Consultancy Series, this book describes the process of designing a theatre, from the initial decision to build through to opening night. Michael Mell's book provides a step-by-step guide to the design and construction of performing arts facilities. Chapters discuss: assembling your team, selecting an architect, different construction methods, the architectural design process, construction of the theatre, theatrical systems and equipment, the stage, backstage, the auditorium, ADA requirements and the lobby. Each chapter clearly describes what to expect and how to avoid surprises. It is a must-read for architects, planners, performing arts groups, educators and anyone who may be considering building or renovating a theatre.

Carry on Fading *Francis Reid 216pp* **£20.00** ISBN: 9781904031642
This is a record of five of the best years of the author's life. Years so good that the only downside is the pangs of guilt at enjoying such contentment in a world full of misery induced by greed, envy and imposed ideologies. Fortunately Francis' DNA is high on luck, optimism and blessing counting.

Case Studies in Crowd Management
Chris Kemp, Iain Hill, Mick Upton, Mark Hamilton 206pp **£16.95**
ISBN: 9781904031482
This important work has been compiled from a series of research projects carried out by the staff of the Centre for Crowd Management and Security Studies at Buckinghamshire Chilterns University College (now Bucks New University), and seminar work carried out in Berlin and Groningen with partner Yourope. It includes case studies, reports and a crowd management safety plan for a major outdoor rock concert, safe management of rock concerts utilising a triple barrier safety system and pan-European Health & Safety Issues.

Case Studies in Crowd Management, Security and Business Continuity
Chris Kemp, Patrick Smith 274pp **£24.95** ISBN: 9781904031635
The creation of good case studies to support work in progress and to give answers to those seeking guidance in their quest to come to terms with perennial questions is no easy task. The first Case Studies in Crowd Management book focused mainly on a series of festivals and events that had a number of issues which required solving. This book focuses on a series of events that had major issues that impacted on the every day delivery of the events researched.

Close Protection – The Softer Skills *Geoffrey Padgham 132pp* **£11.95**
ISBN: 9781904031390
This is the first educational book in a new 'Security Series' for Entertainment Technology Press, and it coincides with the launch of the new 'Protective Security Management' Foundation Degree at Buckinghamshire Chilterns University College (now Bucks New University). The author is a former full-career Metropolitan Police Inspector from New Scotland Yard with 27 years' experience of close protection (CP). For 22 of those years he specialised in operations and senior management duties with the Royalty Protection Department at Buckingham Palace, followed by five years in the private security industry specialising in CP training design and delivery. His wealth of protection experience comes across throughout the text, which incorporates sound advice and exceptional practical guidance, subtly separating fact from fiction. This publication is an excellent form of reference material for experienced operatives, students and trainees.

A Comparative Study of Crowd Behaviour at Two Major Music Events
Chris Kemp, Iain Hill, Mick Upton 78pp **£7.95** ISBN: 9781904031253
A compilation of the findings of reports made at two major live music concerts, and in particular crowd behaviour, which is followed from ingress to egress.

Control Freak *Wayne Howell 270pp* **£28.95** ISBN: 9781904031550
Control Freak is the second book by Wayne Howell. It provides an in depth study of DMX512 and the new RDM (Remote Device Management) standards. The book is aimed at both users and developers and provides a wealth of real world information based on the author's twenty year experience of lighting control.

Copenhagen Opera House *Richard Brett and John Offord 272pp* **£32.00**
ISBN: 9781904031420
Completed in a little over three years, the Copenhagen Opera House opened with a royal gala performance on 15th January 2005. Built on a spacious brown-field site, the building is a landmark venue and this book provides the complete technical background story to an opera house set to become a benchmark for future design and planning. Sixteen chapters by relevant experts involved with the project cover everything from the planning of the auditorium and studio stage, the stage engineering, stage lighting and control and architectural lighting through to acoustic design and sound technology plus technical summaries.

Cue 80 *Francis Reid 310pp* **£17.95** ISBN: 9781904031659
Although Francis Reid's work in theatre has been visual rather than verbal, writing has provided crucial support. Putting words on paper has been the way in which he organised and clarified his thoughts. And in his self-confessed absence of drawing skills, writing has helped him find words to communicate his visual thinking in discussions with the rest of the creative team. As a by-product, this process of searching for the right words to help formulate and analyse ideas has resulted in half-a-century of articles in theatre journals. Cue 80 is an anthology of these articles and is released in celebration of Francis' 80th birthday.

The DMX 512-A Handbook – Design and Implementation of DMX Enabled Products and Networks *James Eade 150pp* **£13.95** ISBN: 9781904031727
This guidebook was originally conceived as a guide to the new DMX512-A standard on behalf of the ESTA Controls Protocols Working Group (CPWG). It has subsequently been updated and is aimed at all levels of reader from technicians working with or servicing equipment in the field as well as manufacturers looking to build in DMX control to their lighting products. It also gives thorough guidance to consultants and designers looking to design DMX networks.

Electric Shadows: an Introduction to Video and Projection on Stage *Nick Moran 234pp* **£23.95** ISBN: 9781904031734
Electric Shadows aims to guide the emerging video designer through the many simple and difficult technical and aesthetic choices and decisions he or she has to make in taking their design from outline idea through to realisation. The main body of the book takes the reader through the process of deciding what content will be projected onto what screen or screens to make the best overall production design. The book will help you make electric shadows that capture the attention of your audience, to help you tell your stories in just the way you want.

Electrical Safety for Live Events *Marco van Beek 98pp* **£16.95** ISBN: 9781904031284
This title covers electrical safety regulations and good practise pertinent to the entertainment industries and includes some basic electrical theory as well as clarifying the "do's and don't's" of working with electricity.

Entertainment in Production Volume 1: 1994-1999 *Rob Halliday 254pp* **£24.95**
ISBN: 9781904031512

Entertainment in Production Volume 2: 2000-2006 *Rob Halliday 242poo* £24.95
ISBN: 9781904031529

Rob Halliday has a dual career as a lighting designer/programmer and author and in these two volumes he provides the intriguing but comprehensive technical background stories behind the major musical productions and other notable projects spanning the period 1994 to 2005. Having been closely involved with the majority of the events described, the author is able to present a first-hand and all-encompassing portrayal of how many of the major shows across the past decade came into being. From *Oliver!* and *Miss Saigon* to *Mamma Mia!* and *Mary Poppins*, here the complete technical story unfolds. The books, which are profusely illustrated, are in large part an adapted selection of articles that first appeared in the magazine *Lighting&Sound International*.

Entertainment Technology Yearbook 2008 *John Offord 220pp* **£14.95**
ISBN: 9781904031543

The Entertainment Technology Yearbook 2008 covers the year 2007 and includes picture coverage of major industry exhibitions in Europe compiled from the pages of Entertainment Technology magazine and the etnow.com website, plus articles and pictures of production, equipment and project highlights of the year.

The Exeter Theatre Fire *David Anderson 202pp* **£24.95** ISBN: 9781904031130

This title is a fascinating insight into the events that led up to the disaster at the Theatre Royal, Exeter, on the night of September 5th 1887. The book details what went wrong, and the lessons that were learned from the event.

Fading Light – A Year in Retirement *Francis Reid 134pp* **£14.95**
ISBN: 9781904031352

Francis Reid, the lighting industry's favourite author, describes a full year in retirement. "Old age is much more fun than I expected," he says. Fading Light describes visits and experiences to the author's favourite theatres and opera houses, places of relaxation and re-visits to scholarly institutions.

Focus on Lighting Technology *Richard Cadena 120pp* **£17.95** ISBN: 9781904031147

This concise work unravels the mechanics behind modern performance lighting and appeals to designers and technicians alike. Packed with clear, easy-to-read diagrams, the book provides excellent explanations behind the technology of performance lighting.

The Followspot Guide *Nick Mobsby 450pp* **£28.95** ISBN: 9781904031499

The first in ETP's Equipment Series, Nick Mobsby's Followspot Guide tells you everything you need to know about followspots, from their history through to maintenance and usage. Its pages include a technical specification of 193 followspots from historical to the latest versions from major manufacturers.

From Ancient Rome to Rock 'n' Roll – a Review of the UK Leisure Security Industry
Mick Upton 198pp **£14.95** ISBN: 9781904031505
From stewarding, close protection and crowd management through to his engagement as a senior consultant Mick Upton has been ever present in the events industry. A founder of ShowSec International in 1982 he was its chairman until 2000. The author has led the way on training within the sector. He set up the ShowSec Training Centre and has acted as a consultant at the Bramshill Police College. He has been prominent in the development of courses at Buckinghamshire New University where he was awarded a Doctorate in 2005. Mick has received numerous industry awards. His book is a personal account of the development and professionalism of the sector across the past 50 years.

Gobos for Image Projection *Michael Hall and Julie Harper 176pp* **£25.95**
ISBN: 9781904031628
In this first published book dedicated totally to the gobo, the authors take the reader through from the history of projection to the development of the present day gobo. And there is broad practical advice and ample reference information to back it up. A feature of the work is the inclusion, interspersed throughout the text, of comment and personal experience in the use and application of gobos from over 25 leading lighting designers worldwide.

Health and Safety Aspects in the Live Music Industry *Chris Kemp, Iain Hill 300pp*
£30.00 ISBN: 9781904031222
This major work includes chapters on various safety aspects of live event production and is written by specialists in their particular areas of expertise.

Health and Safety Management in the Live Music and Events Industry *Chris Hannam*
480pp **£25.95** ISBN: 9781904031307
This title covers the health and safety regulations and their application regarding all aspects of staging live entertainment events, and is an invaluable manual for production managers and event organisers.

Hearing the Light – 50 Years Backstage *Francis Reid 280pp* **£24.95**
ISBN: 9781904031185
This highly enjoyable memoir delves deeply into the theatricality of the industry. The author's almost fanatical interest in opera, his formative period as lighting designer at Glyndebourne and his experiences as a theatre administrator, writer and teacher make for a broad and unique background.

An Introduction to Rigging in the Entertainment Industry *Chris Higgs 272pp* **£24.95**
ISBN: 9781904031123
This title is a practical guide to rigging techniques and practices and also thoroughly covers safety issues and discusses the implications of working within recommended guidelines and regulations. Second edition revised September 2008.

Let There be Light – Entertainment Lighting Software Pioneers in Conversation
Robert Bell 390pp **£32.00** ISBN: 9781904031246
Robert Bell interviews a distinguished group of software engineers working on
entertainment lighting ideas and products.

Light and Colour Filters *Michael Hall and Eddie Ruffell 286pp* **£23.95**
ISBN: 9781904031598
Written by two acknowledged and respected experts in the field, this book is destined to
become the standard reference work on the subject. The title chronicles the development
and use of colour filters and also describes how colour is perceived and how filters function.
Up-to-date reference tables will help the practitioner make better and more specific choices
of colour.

Lighting for Roméo and Juliette *John Offord 172pp* **£26.95** ISBN: 9781904031161
John Offord describes the making of the Vienna State Opera production from the lighting
designer's viewpoint – from the point where director Jürgen Flimm made his decision not to
use scenery or sets and simply employ the expertise of lighting designer Patrick Woodroffe.

Lighting Systems for TV Studios *Nick Mobsby 570pp* **£45.00** ISBN: 9781904031000
Lighting Systems for TV Studios, now in its second edition, is the first book specifically
written on the subject and has become the 'standard' resource work for studio planning
and design covering the key elements of system design, luminaires, dimming, control,
data networks and suspension systems as well as detailing the infrastructure items such as
cyclorama, electrical and ventilation. TV lighting principles are explained and some history
on TV broadcasting, camera technology and the equipment is provided to help set the scene!
The second edition includes applications for sine wave and distributed dimming, moving
lights, Ethernet and new cool lamp technology.

Lighting Techniques for Theatre-in-the-Round *Jackie Staines 188pp* **£24.95**
ISBN: 9781904031017
Lighting Techniques for Theatre-in-the-Round is a unique reference source for those
working on lighting design for theatre-in-the-round for the first time. It is the first title to be
published specifically on the subject and it also provides some anecdotes and ideas for more
challenging shows, and attempts to blow away some of the myths surrounding lighting in
this format.

Lighting the Diamond Jubilee Concert *Durham Marenghi 102pp* **£19.95**
ISBN: 9781904031673
In this highly personal landmark document the show's lighting designer Durham Marenghi
pays tribute to the team of industry experts who each played an important role in bringing
the Diamond Jubilee Concert to fruition, both for television and live audiences. The book
contains colour production photography throughout and describes the production processes
and the thinking behind them. In his Foreword, BBC Executive Producer Guy Freeman states:
"Working with the whole lighting team on such a special project was a real treat for me and a
fantastic achievement for them, which the pages of this book give a remarkable insight into."

Lighting the Stage *Francis Reid 120pp* **£14.95** ISBN: 9781904031086
Lighting the Stage discusses the human relationships involved in lighting design – both between people, and between these people and technology. The book is written from a highly personal viewpoint and its 'thinking aloud' approach is one that Francis Reid has used in his writings over the past 30 years.

Miscellany of Lighting and Stagecraft *Michael Hall & Julie Harper 222pp* **£22.95**
ISBN: 9781904031680
This title will help schools, colleges, amateurs, technicians and all those interested in practical theatre and performance to understand, in an entertaining and informative way, the key backstage skills. Within its pages, numerous professionals share their own special knowledge and expertise, interspersed with diversions of historic interest and anecdotes from those practising at the front line of the industry. As a result, much of the advice and skills set out have not previously been set in print. The editors' intention with this book is to provide a Miscellany that is not ordered or categorised in strict fashion, but rather encourages the reader to flick through or dip into it, finding nuggets of information and anecdotes to entertain, inspire and engender curiosity – also to invite further research or exploration and generally encourage people to enter the industry and find out for themselves.

Mr Phipps' Theatre *Mark Jones, John Pick 172pp* £17.95 ISBN: 9781904031383
Mark Jones and John Pick describe "The Sensational Story of Eastbourne's Royal Hippodrome" – formerly Eastbourne Theatre Royal. An intriguing narrative, the book sets the story against a unique social history of the town. Peter Longman, former director of The Theatres Trust, provides the Foreword.

Northen Lights *Michael Northen 256pp* **£17.95** ISBN: 9781904031666
Many books have been written by famous personalities in the theatre about their lives and work. However this is probably one of the first memoirs by someone who has spent his entire career behind scenes, and not in front of the footlights. As a lighting designer and as consultant to designers and directors, Michael Northen worked through an exciting period of fifty years of theatrical history from the late nineteen thirties in theatres in the UK and abroad, and on productions ranging from Shakespeare, opera and ballet to straight plays, pantomimes and cabaret. This is not a complicated technical text book, but is intended to give an insight into some of the 300 productions in which he had been involved and some of the directors, the designers and backstage staff he have worked with, viewed from a new angle.

Pages From Stages *Anthony Field 204pp* **£17.95** ISBN: 9781904031260
Anthony Field explores the changing style of theatres including interior design, exterior design, ticket and seat prices, and levels of service, while questioning whether the theatre still exists as a place of entertainment for regular theatre-goers.

People, Places, Performances *Remembered by Francis Reid 60pp* **£8.95**
ISBN: 9781904031765
In growing older, the Author has found that memories, rather than featuring the events, increasingly tend to focus on the people who caused them, the places where they happened

and the performances that arose. So Francis Reid has used these categories in endeavouring to compile a brief history of the second half of the twentieth century.

Performing Arts Technical Training Handbook 2013/2014 *ed: John Offord 304pp* **£19.95** ISBN: 9781904031710
Published in association with the ABTT (Association of British Theatre Technicians), this important Handbook, now in its third edition, includes fully detailed and indexed entries describing courses on backstage crafts offered by over 100 universities and colleges across the UK. A completely new research project, with accompanying website, the title also includes articles with advice for those considering a career 'behind the scenes', together with contact information and descriptions of the major organisations involved with industry training – plus details of companies offering training within their own premises.

Practical Dimming *Nick Mobsby 364pp* **£22.95** ISBN: 97819040313444
This important and easy to read title covers the history of electrical and electronic dimming, how dimmers work, current dimmer types from around the world, planning of a dimming system, looking at new sine wave dimming technology and distributed dimming. Integration of dimming into different performance venues as well as the necessary supporting electrical systems are fully detailed. Significant levels of information are provided on the many different forms and costs of potential solutions as well as how to plan specific solutions. Architectural dimming for the likes of hotels, museums and shopping centres is included. Practical Dimming is a companion book to Practical DMX and is designed for all involved in the use, operation and design of dimming systems.

Practical DMX *Nick Mobsby 276pp* **£16.95** ISBN: 9781904031369
In this highly topical and important title the author details the principles of DMX, how to plan a network, how to choose equipment and cables, with data on products from around the world, and how to install DMX networks for shows and on a permanently installed basis. The easy style of the book and the helpful fault finding tips, together with a review of different DMX testing devices provide an ideal companion for all lighting technicians and system designers. An introduction to Ethernet and Canbus networks are provided as well as tips on analogue networks and protocol conversion. It also includes a chapter on Remote Device Management.

A Practical Guide to Health and Safety in the Entertainment Industry
Marco van Beek 120pp **£14.95** ISBN: 9781904031048
This book is designed to provide a practical approach to Health and Safety within the Live Entertainment and Event industry. It gives industry-pertinent examples, and seeks to break down the myths surrounding Health and Safety.

Production Management *Joe Aveline 134pp* **£17.95** ISBN: 9781904031109
Joe Aveline's book is an in-depth guide to the role of the Production Manager, and includes real-life practical examples and 'Aveline's Fables' – anecdotes of his experiences with real messages behind them.

Rigging for Entertainment: Regulations and Practice *Chris Higgs 156pp* **£19.95**
ISBN: 9781904031215
Continuing where he left off with his highly successful An Introduction to Rigging in the
Entertainment Industry, Chris Higgs' second title covers the regulations and use of equipment
in greater detail.

Rock Solid Ethernet *Wayne Howell 304pp* **£23.95** ISBN: 9781904031697
Now in its third completely revised and reset edition, Rock Solid Ethernet is aimed
specifically at specifiers, installers and users of entertainment industry systems, and will give
the reader a thorough grounding in all aspects of computer networks, whatever industry they
may work in. The inclusion of historical and technical 'sidebars' make for an enjoyable as
well as an informative read.

Sixty Years of Light Work *Fred Bentham 450pp* **£26.95** ISBN: 9781904031079
This title is an autobiography of one of the great names behind the development of modern
stage lighting equipment and techniques. It includes a complete facsimile of the famous
Strand Electric Catalogue of May 1936 – a reference work in itself.

Sound for the Stage *Patrick Finelli 218pp* **£24.95** ISBN: 9781904031154
Patrick Finelli's thorough manual covering all aspects of live and recorded sound for
performance is a complete training course for anyone interested in working in the field of
stage sound, and is a must for any student of sound.

Stage Automation *Anton Woodward 128pp* **£12.95** ISBN: 9781904031567
The purpose of this book is to explain the stage automation techniques used in modern
theatre to achieve some of the spectacular visual effects seen in recent years. The book
is targeted at automation operators, production managers, theatre technicians, stage
engineering machinery manufacturers and theatre engineering students. Topics are covered
in sufficient detail to provide an insight into the thought processes that the stage automation
engineer has to consider when designing a control system to control stage machinery in a
modern theatre. The author has worked on many stage automation projects and developed
the award-winning Impressario stage automation system.

Stage Lighting Design in Britain: The Emergence of the Lighting Designer, 1881-1950
Nigel Morgan 300pp **£17.95** ISBN: 9781904031345
This title sets out to ascertain the main course of events and the controlling factors that
determined the emergence of the theatre lighting designer in Britain, starting with the
introduction of incandescent electric light to the stage, and ending at the time of the first
public lighting design credits around 1950. The book explores the practitioners, equipment,
installations and techniques of lighting design.

Stage Lighting for Theatre Designers *Nigel Morgan 124pp* **£17.95**
ISBN: 9781904031192
This is an updated second edition of Nigel Morgan's popular book for students of theatre
design – outlining all the techniques of stage lighting design.

Technical Marketing Techniques   *David Brooks, Andy Collier, Steve Norman 160pp*
£24.95 ISBN: 9781904031031
Technical Marketing is a novel concept, defined and elaborated by the authors of this book, with business-to-business companies competing in fast developing technical product sectors.

Technical Standards for Places of Entertainment   *ABTT 354pp A4*   **£45.00**
ISBN: 9781904031703
Technical Standards for Places of Entertainment details the necessary physical standards required for entertainment venues. Known in the industry as the "Yellow Book" the latest completely revised edition was first published in June 2013.

Theatre Engineering and Stage Machinery   *Toshiro Ogawa 332pp*   **£30.00**
ISBN: 9781904031024
Theatre Engineering and Stage Machinery is a unique reference work covering every aspect of theatrical machinery and stage technology in global terms, and across the complete historical spectrum. Revised February 2007.

Theatre Lighting in the Age of Gas   *Terence Rees 232pp*   **£24.95**
ISBN: 9781904031178
Entertainment Technology Press has republished this valuable historic work previously produced by the Society for Theatre Research in 1978. Theatre Lighting in the Age of Gas investigates the technological and artistic achievements of theatre lighting engineers from the 1700s to the late Victorian period.

Theatre Space: A Rediscovery Reported   *Francis Reid 238pp*   **£19.95**
ISBN: 9781904031437
In the post-war world of the 1950s and 60s, the format of theatre space became a matter for a debate that aroused passions of an intensity unknown before or since. The proscenium arch was clearly identified as the enemy, accused of forming a barrier to disrupt the relations between the actor and audience. An uneasy fellow-traveller at the time, Francis Reid later recorded his impressions whilst enjoying performances or working in theatres old and new and this book is an important collection of his writings in various theatrical journals from 1969-2001 including his contribution to the Cambridge Guide to the Theatre in 1988. It reports some of the flavour of the period when theatre architecture was rediscovering its past in a search to establish its future.

The Theatres and Concert Halls of Fellner and Helmer   *Michael Sell 244pp*   **£23.95**
ISBN: 9781904031772
This is the first British study of the works of the prolific Fellner and Helmer Atelier which was active from 1871-1914 during which time they produced over 80 theatre designs and are second in quantity only to Frank Matcham, to whom reference is made.
This period is one of great change as a number of serious theatre fires which included Nice and Vienna had the effect of the introduction of safety legislation which affected theatre design. This study seeks to show how Fellner and Helmer and Frank Matcham dealt with this increasing safety legislation, in particular the way in which safety was built into their

new three part theatres equipped with iron stages, safety curtains, electricity and appropriate access and egress and, in the Vienna practice, how this was achieved across 13 countries.

Theatres of Achievement *John Higgins 302pp* **£29.95** ISBN: 9781904031376
John Higgins affectionately describes the history of 40 distinguished UK theatres in a personal tribute, each uniquely illustrated by the author. Completing each profile is colour photography by Adrian Eggleston.

Theatric Tourist *Francis Reid 220pp* **£19.95** ISBN: 9781904031468
Theatric Tourist is the delightful story of Francis Reid's visits across more than 50 years to theatres, theatre museums, performances and even movie theme parks. In his inimitable style, the author involves the reader within a personal experience of venues from the Legacy of Rome to theatres of the Renaissance and Eighteenth Century Baroque and the Gustavian Theatres of Stockholm. His performance experiences include Wagner in Beyreuth, the Pleasures of Tivoli and Wayang in Singapore. This is a 'must have' title for those who are as "incurably stagestruck" as the author.

Through the Viewfinder *Jeremy Hoare 276pp* **£21.95** ISBN:: 9781904031574
Do you want to be a top television cameraman? Well this is going to help!
Through the Viewfinder is aimed at media students wanting to be top professional television cameramen – but it will also be of interest to anyone who wants to know what goes on behind the cameras that bring so much into our homes.
The author takes his own opinionated look at how to operate a television camera based on 23 years' experience looking through many viewfinders for a major ITV network company. Based on interviews with people he has worked with, all leaders in the profession, the book is based on their views and opinions and is a highly revealing portrait of what happens behind the scenes in television production from a cameraman's point of view.

Walt Disney Concert Hall – The Backstage Story *Patricia MacKay & Richard Pilbrow 250pp* **£28.95** ISBN: 9781904031239
Spanning the 16-year history of the design and construction of the Walt Disney Concert Hall, this book provides a fresh and detailed behind the scenes story of the design and technology from a variety of viewpoints. This is the first book to reveal the "process" of the design of a concert hall.

Yesterday's Lights – A Revolution Reported *Francis Reid 352pp* **£26.95**
ISBN: 9781904031321
Set to help new generations to be aware of where the art and science of theatre lighting is coming from – and stimulate a nostalgia trip for those who lived through the period, Francis Reid's latest book has over 350 pages dedicated to the task, covering the 'revolution' from the fifties through to the present day. Although this is a highly personal account of the development of lighting design and technology and he admits that there are 'gaps', you'd be hard put to find anything of significance missing.

Go to www.etbooks.co.uk for full details of above titles and secure online ordering facilities. Most books also available for Kindle.